ENTERTAINING ANGELS
Engaging the Unseen Realm

by RANDY CLARK
with TIMOTHY BERRY
ANNIE BYRNE
CHRIS ISHAK

Entertaining Angels: Engaging the Unseen Realm.
First Edition, October 2008, Second Printing 2011.
© Copyright 2008 Randy Clark.
All rights reserved.

Edited by: Bob Baynard.

Apostolic Network of Global Awakening
1451 Clark St
Mechanicsburg, PA 17055

Disclaimer: Website references given are correct at time of publication, but may change over time. We cannot guarantee their continued accuracy or availability.

ISBN: 0-9818454-3-6
ISBN: 978-0-9818454-3-2

www.globalawakening.com

TABLE OF CONTENTS

INTRODUCTION

As an avid student of church history, I am aware that there are trends and seasons for certain areas of interest within the church. A particular topic will surface and for a while, it seems that is all we hear about, the latest buzzword or phrase. The pendulum will swing sometimes to the extreme and then swing back either toward a more balanced view or to the opposite extreme where no one seems willing to address the issue or concern any more. The whole study of angels is one of the more recent hot topics. For a while it felt like everyone was talking about angels. There were even several popular television shows that pursued the theme, probably most notably, Touched by an Angel. All sorts of angel jewelry showed up on retail shelves and any number of books about these mysterious heavenly beings were published, both from Christian and non-Christian perspectives. The pendulum has now begun to swing back. But all this interest has left in its wake a great deal of misunderstanding and misinformation regarding angels. As I already suggested might happen, there has been some backlash to the point where some folks either want to avoid the topic or become critical of those who do raise it.

So here is yet another book on angels. Why? We feel that there is plenty of truth about angels in the Bible that needs to be emphasized to help people overcome misconceptions and come to understand that God created angels for multiple purposes. As we study what has been revealed, we see that these heavenly messengers provide invaluable assistance to ᴐse of us who believe. Also, we can understand the unseen heavenly realm by studying the creatures who inhabit it. While this current volume will by no means represent an exhaustive study of the subject, it is our hope that every reader will come away with the eyes of their understanding opened to comprehend and experience more fully all that God has for us to introduce His Kingdom to our world.

I've started off the book with a message about how I came to understand the helpful role that angels play when we are praying for healing. It ends with a chapter full of suggestions about how you can become activated in experiencing angelic assistance in your life and ministry. In between, we spend time looking at many of the biblical references about angels to see how they are revealed to us. We also add many personal stories of modern day dealings with heavenly beings to see what we can learn about the hows and whys of encountering angelic messengers. All this reminds us of the words of Jesus, "The Kingdom of heaven is at hand." It remains for us to grow in the ways of God so that we become carriers of His Kingdom and His Presence wherever we find ourselves, so that all may come to the knowledge of our King!

Finally, let me include a word of thanks. This book would not have been possible without the inspired efforts of my faithful interns: Timothy Berry, Annie Byrne and Chris Ishak. I offer heartfelt appreciation for your long hours of study and writing.

Randy Clark
Mechanicsburg, Pennsylvania
September 2008

CHAPTER 1

OPEN HEAVEN: UNDERSTANDING ANGELIC INTERVENTION

I do not believe that I could have received this message had I not left the country. A lot of what I am writing about grew out of my experience in Brazil. It grew out of an encounter or discussion in Birmingham, England, and then as these experiences came, I was able to see what was in the Bible all along but just hadn't registered. It didn't make sense. It didn't have power; it was just words. But out of what occurred, I found that the experience was scriptural and began to see things I hadn't seen before. In this teaching on the Open Heaven, I will be mentioning quite a bit about angels but the teaching is not about angels. It is about all that has been purchased for us by the cross of Jesus Christ and what he died to make available for us. It is a fuller understanding of all that the cross merited and how it opened up heaven. We will be looking at Genesis 28 and the dream of Jacob, which I believe is one of the most profound prophetic dreams recorded in the Bible. It was both looking to and fulfilled in the new covenant in the cross of Jesus Christ.

DEALING WITH OLD WINESKINS

When I first began hearing about some of the material I am writing about, I didn't accept it. It was too weird. I didn't know what to do with it. So, I just put it on the back burner. I didn't even want to deal with it. It began for me in 1995 when I was in Birmingham, England. I had the opportunity to meet with one of the men who had been a hero of mine. I had read about his life eleven years earlier (1984) in John Wimber's book on signs, wonders and church growth and had wanted to meet him since then. I had heard about his stories and I said, "God, I would love to meet Omar Cabrera, the famous pioneer evangelist in Argentina." I had my opportunity. We were in this little private hotel and he and I began talking. I asked him this question: "Omar, you are a famous evangelist and I am just getting started and don't know what I am doing. I have just been caught up in this thing and need wisdom. Is there anything you can teach me that would help me where I could see more happening in my meetings?" He looked and said, "Yes". I said, "What!" He said, "Randy, I have never understood why you North Americans who understand the Holy Spirit, you understand the gifts of the spirit, you ask for the Holy Spirit to come and you want to move in the gifts of the spirit, but why don't you pray for God to send his angels to your meetings." Now I have seven years of theological training. My major and minor and all my electives in college were in religion. Then, I went to seminary because by the time I graduated from that liberal college, I didn't believe enough to stay in the ministry. While in seminary I tried to play the Devil's advocate hoping that the conservative professors I had chosen would destroy those liberal arguments that I had gotten in college. The difficult thing was there weren't very many conservative professors to ask. But, because of my theological training and understanding of the attributes of God, which are the big O's - omnipotence, omniscience and omnipresence, if he is omnipotent, he has all power; if he is omniscient, he knows all things; and if he is omnipresent, he is everywhere at once. If you have a God like that, why do you need help? I mean, if you have a God like that why would you need an angel? I have read from church history that if one gets to talking about angels, that is where it can get weird and off balance really easily. Therefore, I was a little reticent to even consider the subject. I just didn't have any place in my evangelical theology for asking God for angels. I didn't have any room for angels. To me that was kind of a superfluous thing. It was something peripheral, that wasn't central and core to the gospel. It took away from intimacy with God. I didn't want any intermediaries between God and me. I had lots of things that just kind of rose up in mind about why I didn't even want to think about that. So, I didn't. And so that part of the discussion was put on the back burner.

LESSONS FROM HISTORY

When I was in New Zealand, a church elder gave me a little book. There were three books written by Owen Jorgensen about William Branham called: *The Life of the Supernatural.* If you do not own these books, you ought to. If you need to go sell your car, take out a line of equity in your home, or whatever you need to do to purchase those books, do so. Only the first three were completed when I started to read them. Because I have read a lot about church history, I knew that Branham ended up at the end of his life in deception but that doesn't mean the great miracles that took place in the early part of his life were invalid. As I read these books, I literally wept. I actually wouldn't even put one down while I was getting my haircut. I said this is unbelievable. I learned more about a man who was trying to learn how to cooperate with God from that material than from any other book that I had read. This was happening and I didn't understand it or know how to cooperate with it. I didn't know what to do if I had a vision. What do you do with it? As I watched him learn and make mistakes, I learned a lot. Also, it was great reading. It's a great story. My heart broke several times as I saw the brokenness of this man in his struggling with God. At that time if anyone had experienced anything like this, pastors would tell you it was the Devil instead of God. I also noticed that the angelic played a big role in his greatest miracles. So, there's another signpost. By the way, I could hardly wait until the rest of the series was finished. There are five available now. I am sure the next one, which is going to be the last part of his life, will be off the wall when he gets into heresy. But it is written from a supportive kind of Branhamite. As my friend Bill Johnson suggests, we want to read it so we can learn how he became deceived. Hopefully, the next book in the series will give us some insight. After reading the Branham books, I started reading the Bible and suddenly, because I was thinking about this now, I was seeing things that previously I had been overlooking. My problem was this: If I have the Holy Spirit, why do I need angels? Have you ever thought about that? If you have the Holy Spirit, why do you even need any angelic intervention? In my Bible reading I reached some familiar portions about Jesus' life. After he was baptized in the Jordan River and received the Holy Spirit, he was lead by the Spirit into the wilderness where he was tempted by the Devil. After that time the Father sent angels to strengthen him. Who? Jesus! Here's a man who was the eternal Son of God, who became flesh, full of the Holy Spirit, born of the Spirit and conceived of the Spirit. If there was anyone who was perfectly living by the Spirit, it was Jesus the Son of God. Yet the Bible says Jesus was strengthened by angels. Now that got my curiosity up! In the Garden of Gethsemane after Jesus prayed that great prayer of agony, once again the Bible says an angel came and strengthened him. I began to think, there is something wrong here. If even the Son of God had angels come and help him, wouldn't I also need angels to come and help me? Who do I think I am? Then, I read in the Bible that an angel came and let Peter out of jail. As I continued reading the Bible, Philip was preaching a great revival and was lead by both the Spirit and angelic activity to go down to Gaza. Then, John received a revelation and didn't know how to understand all he was seeing. So God arranged for an angel to help John interpret what he was seeing in the revelation. Then I read where the Apostle Paul was in a ship that was about to go down and an angel came to strengthen and encourage him. The angel told Paul what to do so that no lives would be lost. I said: Jesus, Paul, Peter, Philip and John were all in the Bible and visited by angels. The New Testament is basically full of cooperation between the Holy Spirit and angelic beings. Why have I have been so blind and resistant to this when it was so obviously present in the Bible. I then began to be more open to this thinking.

I remembered that in January 1994, at the first few weeks of the outpouring in the Toronto revival a young girl named Heather, who was 14 years old, came to me for prayer. She was severely dyslexic and reading at the second grade level in the eighth grade. I prayed for her and she was out under the Spirit for about 45 minutes or longer. During this time she had a vision. When the girl came to, she said she saw herself being operated on by an angel that rewired her head. Her mother and father were pastors in the Vineyard in Hopkinsville, Kentucky. Their career before pastoring was as mental health professionals. She asked her mother to get her a book. Previously she could hardly do math at all and it was hard for her to read. She began to read the book easily. It clicked. Something had been rewired in her head. Some years later, she was at a Healing School and gave her testimony. She graduated fifth in her high school class. She was also healed of allergies and some other stuff. Heather's best friend, Monica, was dyslexic also. When Heather returned home from being healed, she went up to Monica and said "Monica, Jesus is going to heal you." She did not tell Monica about her healing, she just prayed for her friend. Sometime later, Monica said, "I had a vision. I saw an angel come and rewire my head." Monica was healed of dyslexia too. Later, the girls realized that both had the same vision. Suddenly, I was realizing that there was more here than what I originally thought.

I come from a Baptist background and sometimes God uses things from my Baptist training to get a point across. You know God has to deal with what he's got in you. He has to use your building block material to get messages to you. If you have a Methodist background, he will probably give you some Methodist stories. If you have a Baptist background, he'll give you some Baptist stories. God reminded me of two things that happened to me in the past. When I was in Seminary, one of my favorite professors, Dr. Wayne Ward, was one of the few conservative teachers at the Seminary at that time. His teaching fellow, who was the guy that did all the grading for the professor, gave a lecture one day and told this true story from his life. This was really bizarre because at that time the Southern Baptist Seminary was very liberal theologically. This guy said,

I was in Uganda and captured by soldiers that heard there were white mercenaries in this region. I was captured along with a group of mercenaries. I could not clear up the confusion that I was a missionary not a mercenary. So, we were all to be shot in the morning. I could not convince them that I was not part of the mercenary group. They were going to kill me in the morning. I had a pocket New Testament and thought I might as well lead them all to the Lord. So, I shared the gospel with the mercenaries and many of them accepted the Lord. I just knew I was going to be killed in the morning. Then, somebody came into the jail where I was being held and told me that at a certain time the door is going to open and you should go out and go down around the corner where you will find a canoe. Get in the canoe and go across the lake. There will be somebody there to get you out. I never saw that person before and never saw him afterwards. Then at a certain time around 2 o'clock in the morning, it happened just like the guy said. I got away. My parents were missionaries in Africa. Later when I was with them, they asked me if I recalled what I was doing on a specific night. The date they gave was the day before I was to be killed the next morning. I said, "Yes Mom and Dad, I remember where I was on that night and why do you ask?" My Mother said, "Your father and I were awakened from our sleep by the Holy Spirit and knew you were in trouble. We prayed under a great burden until the burden lifted. We were always curious as

5

to what was going on in your life. Could you tell us?" I then told them. "I was delivered from that prison by an angel of the Lord and no one can convince me otherwise."

The other illustration I remember from my Baptist background, was about one of the first Protestant missionaries of the modern missionary era, excluding the Moravians. He was a Baptist named William Carey, a shoe cobbler. He got up in this big Baptist meeting in front of the leaders and said, "I feel like God is calling me to go preach the gospel to the heathen in India." Then, one of the most scholarly, well trained theological pastors of the Baptist stood up and said, "Young man, sit down, God does not need you to reach the heathen of India. God is sovereign. God can do anything he wants." Of course, both of those men were right. God can do anything he wants. But you see there is a big difference between the philosophical possibilities of what God can do and the ways God has chosen. William Carey was right also. He was being called of God to go to India and preach the gospel to the heathen. All of a sudden, it dawned on me that my problem with angels was that God doesn't need them. He can do anything he wants. That was the theologian's problem with William Carey and with missionaries. He was saying God doesn't need you. He is sovereign and can do anything he wants. That's the issue. God wanted to create angels. He didn't need them. He just wanted to create them. God wanted to create human beings. He didn't need us. He just wanted to do it. It's the same thing. Humans are the Army and angels are the Air Force. We both need to get our act together. That's what we are going to consider.

MORE PROPHETIC INSIGHT

There is one other thing about how this was opened to me. In 1994, I was in Charlotte, North Carolina praying for about 400 pastors and wives. Mahesh and Bonnie Chavda were there. As I was praying, most were falling down—some were trembling, some were weeping, some were laughing and some were crying. Bonnie motioned for me from where she was on the floor and said, "Do you want me to tell you what I am seeing?" I knew that Mahesh was a New Testament evangelist with a healing gift and Bonnie was quite prophetic. I have always been intrigued with what I feel to be genuine prophetic-type people. I said to Bonnie, "Yes, what do you see?" She said:

When you started praying, instantly hundreds of angels came into this room and started going around touching the people. The angels had pouches on. When you would go up and start praying for somebody, the angel would come right up beside you and reach in his pouch. There was like this anointing strength the angel would put into the spirit of the man or woman to strengthen them. After awhile, three big angels came in that were about three feet taller than the others. The first angels were about your size. But these guys were about three feet taller and had a greater, brighter glow about them because they had been closer to the throne. They didn't have pouches and they weren't strengthening. You see they had come with a different assignment and different purpose. They had a scroll and a stamp. When you would begin to pray for somebody a big angel would come along beside you and open up the scroll that had been given to him in heaven about that person's life. As I watched him, that angel was declaring into the heavens, into the spirit realm, God's destiny over this person. Then after the angel made the declaration, he would pull out this stamp and stamp this person on the forehead.

Now this is my opinion, not theology, but I believe when we prophesy, we declare and come into agreement with what is already being declared by the angel of the Lord from heaven's throne. The gift of prophecy allows the believer to reveal what God is saying in the heavenlies about a person. Throughout Scripture, God often uses angels to declare his purposes and deliver His messages. The stamp placed on the people's forehead is found in the book of Revelation chapter 7, where those who did not receive the mark of the antichrist were stamped by an angel with the mark of Christ.

ANGELS: ON PURPOSE

All of that happened in my life before I really got this message. Then the rest of the message really came alive and became more than theology a little later on in Brazil. It was only after this experience that I got the courage to share this message. Now I feel like there are times that God illustrates the teaching.

We will begin at Genesis 28:10 through 12,

¹⁰Jacob left Beersheba and set out for Haran. ¹¹When he reached a certain place, he stopped for the night because the sun had set. Taking one of the stones there, he put it under his head and lay down to sleep. ¹²He had a dream in which he saw a stairway resting on the earth, with its top reaching to heaven, and the angels of God were ascending and descending on it.

Say that to yourself: Ascending and descending on it. On what? The ladder if you're using King James, the stairway if you're using the NIV. In Portuguese, it is *escala*, where we get the word escalator. By the way, I thought of a new name for the church but nobody thinks I'm serious. Maybe it's too far out to do but this is the name I thought about for my church: The Stairway to Heaven. Of course, I would like to take a song by Led Zeppelin, change the words to it and keep the tune. But that may be a little bit edgy for some people because there is an interest in the subject; The Stairway to Heaven. The angels were ascending and descending on the ladder, which reached from the earth into heaven.

¹³There above it stood the Lord and he said: "I am the Lord, the God of your father Abraham and the God of Isaac. I will give you and your descendants the land on which you are lying. ¹⁴Your descendants will be like the dust of the earth, and you will spread out to the west and to the east, to the north and to the south. All peoples on earth will be blessed through you and your offspring. ¹⁵I am with you and will watch over you wherever you go, and I will bring you back to this land. I will not leave you until I have done what I have promised you." ¹⁶When Jacob awoke from his sleep, he thought, "Surely the Lord is in this place and I was not aware of it." ¹⁷He was afraid and said, "How awesome is this place! This is none other than the house of God; this is the gate of heaven" (Gen 10:13-17).

I have told you before that I grew up in a very prejudiced era when things weren't as good as they are now, ecumenically speaking. I grew up reading J.R. Graves, that famous landmark scholar of the Southern Baptist Convention who traced Southern Baptist history all the way back through every heretical group there ever was to John the Baptist. Now I say that with tongue in cheek because if you go back and look at those groups, many of them had really, really weird views and were actually heretical in many of their views. But for the Baptists, the important thing was they weren't part of the Catholic Church. The doctrine was: Baptists aren't really Protestant because we never were part of the Protestant movement. We can trace our history all the way back to John the Baptist. We were looking for authority. When you don't have much to stand on, just get louder. It was a time where we said, now you know the Methodists are not really churches. The Methodists are a religious society because they don't have their doctrine right. Of course, there were lots of things said in that era about the Catholic Church. And they were saying terrible things about us too. At least, we weren't burning and killing each other at that time. It was somewhat better than it had been. I've had opportunities to preach in a former Church of Christ. When I was a kid growing up, the Church of Christ guy from my little town would say on radio, "I want you to know that we are the real church. You will not find the word Baptist Church, you will not find the word Methodist Church, and you will not find the word Nazarene Church." You will find in the Bible if you really want to be biblical and want to be in a real church, there is only one name and it is the Church of Christ. I would like to just make a suggestion. Maybe more important than whether we got our policy down right, our mode of baptism down, our view of apostolic succession down, our view of instruments and non-instruments right or wrong, and maybe more than some of these doctrinal, political, governmental things, why don't we just say that a New Testament church should be like the gateway to heaven. It should be the place where there is such a presence and awareness of God that some people become afraid because the beginning of wisdom is the fear of the Lord. Why can't it be that way? We focus more on whether or not we are pleasing to his presence rather than those other things. Isn't it possible that we have made the commandments of God of no effect at times by our own traditions? I am starting, I'm sure there will be some things that when we get to heaven, God is going to clarify for me and say you missed it on that one. But you know, I don't care because God knows my heart and that I am trying to follow him. I just want to love him. But, I want my church to be a place where you can experience God regardless of how and when you come. My church in St. Louis was half former Roman Catholics. The first two missionaries we sent out were Greek Orthodox. We had Southern Baptists, Missouri Synod Lutherans, and New Age guys that grew up in bars. One of my worships leaders was a New Age guy we got out of the bar and the other guy was Roman Catholic. What brought us together was the presence of Jesus. If we were invited to minister in a Roman Catholic Church, we thanked God for it. If we were invited to preach in a Methodist Church, we thanked God for it. If we were invited to preach in a Baptist Church, we thanked God for it. I didn't want us to be a place where we find our unity only if we believe the same thing. I wanted us to find our unity because we know the same One. I started my church in the basement of a Southern Baptist home. God brought people to us who had dropped out of church and who weren't really going for traditions. Some were just looking for a place where they could experience the presence of God a little more in their life.

OPEN HEAVEN REALITIES

The angels of God were ascending and descending on it. The subject is the Open Heaven. I will be referring now to John 1:47 through 51.

⁴⁷When Jesus saw Nathanael approaching, he said of him, "Here is a true Israelite, in whom there is nothing false."⁴⁸"How do you know me?" Nathanael asked. Jesus answered, "I saw you while you were still under the fig tree before Philip called you."

⁴⁹Then Nathanael declared, "Rabbi, you are the Son of God; you are the King of Israel."

⁵⁰Jesus said, "You believe because I told you I saw you under the fig tree. You shall see greater things than that." ⁵¹He then added, "I tell you the truth, you shall see heaven open, and the angels of God ascending and descending on the Son of Man."

In the dream of Genesis 28, Jesus is the *Escala*. Jesus is the ladder. Jesus is the stairway. When the cross fell into that hole, Jesus is the one who was crucified and opened heaven. He pierced heaven. From earth toward heaven, it was pierced because he had come down from heaven and was going to return to his Father. Because of what He did through him, the offspring of Abraham, all nations would be blessed. Jesus is the one that says, "...you shall see heaven open ....(Jn 1:51)" Now what is characteristic of an open heaven? When heaven is open, there is activity between heaven's realm and earth's realm. When heaven is open, there are angelic beings ascending and descending. Jesus said to Philip, "I tell you the truth, you shall see heaven open, and the angels of God ascending and descending on the Son of Man." Now the Son of Man was not a humble title like Jesus saying little ole me. The Son of Man was the fulfillment of the prophecy in Daniel 7 where it says, "I saw one coming from the ancient of days like unto the Son of Man." It was a Messianic title. He said:

You shall see ... the angels of God ascending and descending on me because I am the Son of Man of Daniel 7. I am the fulfillment, I am the Messiah and I am the Son of God. I am God become flesh and you are going to see angels ascending and descending on me.

Now, from the Bible I told you the two times that referenced when angels came and visited Jesus. But, this passage says to Nathanael that he is going to see angels ascending and descending on Jesus. We are not told in the Bible when that happened. However, I believe Nathanael saw it because Jesus is God and the Bible says that God is not a man that he should lie. So, we know from that inference that Jesus had these visitations more than the two times that we are told about in scripture because of what he said to Nathanael. We need to realize that Jesus is what this is all about. The open heaven happens because of him. Here is the connection we need to make. We are the body of Christ on the earth today. Where is this open heaven supposed to be? Over us. We should have an understanding that under this open heaven there is angelic activity going on whether we can see it or not. We can understand that this was literally occurring upon the body of Christ both in the historic context of Jesus and it continues to happen now in the life of his body, the church. In other words, we are not left here alone. He said, I will not leave you here alone. He meant he was going to send the Holy Spirit to us. But, I think we have limited so much of the new covenant to our understanding of the contrast and difference of the role the Holy Spirit had between the Old Testament and the New Testament time. I want you to know that there is a greater dimension and outpouring of the Holy Spirit than the Old Testament people ever had. It is the same way when we consider the contrast of involvement of the angelic hosts between the new covenant people and the old covenant people. One of the benefits of the cross of Jesus Christ is this open heaven with the Holy Spirit poured out and angelic activity. Both were a new dimension that came upon us by grace because of what Jesus accomplished at the cross.

CONFIRMATION THROUGH EXPERIENCE

Now turn to Hebrews 1:14.

14Are not all angels ministering spirits sent to serve those who will inherit salvation.

There are a couple of things I want to unpack here. The root of the word ministering is *diakonos*, which is where we get the word deacon, which means someone who comes along and waits upon you and helps you. Therefore, not only is the Holy Spirit the great helper, but all angels are ministering spirits sent from heaven to earth and then back to heaven after serving those of us who will inherit eternal life. God created the angels to carry out his bidding, to worship him and to serve us. In verse 7, he says:

7He makes his angels winds,
his servants flames of fire.

I used to think that was poetry, I really did. I thought: Isn't that pretty. It is even in a poetic form. It was meant to be poetic.

I believed that way until I was in Volta Redonda, Brazil preaching to 3,000 in a tent and in a place where there weren't any windows. I said (speaking metaphorically, poetically), "God send your wind through this place." They told me later that when I said that, the wind blew through and it really encouraged us. Wow! They said to me, "You said send your wind and God did." Wasn't that a nice coincidence? At least that's what I thought.

We then went from there to Goiania, Brazil. In Goiania, I was on my knees worshipping during the worship time when suddenly I felt this really strong wind hit me all at once. I opened my eyes. I thought somebody had twirled by me. Maybe one of the women dancing had twirled around and caught the wind. But nobody was there. Nearby, there was a guy from Atlanta, Georgia, named Mike. I then said, "Mike did you do that?" He said, "What?" I said, "Forget it." It was really getting weird. I thought I was getting weird. I have been in Brazil too long. But then I thought, "God what was that?" I then had this strong impression that God had sent his angels. I said, "Lord, how can I know that's not my head talking to me but really you? I mean if that was really you, I would like to know it. How can I know?" I got another impression to tell the people that angels are here and they are going to feel wind come across their face or pressure come on their shoulders or head. When they do, have them stand up and I will heal them without a word. Nobody will have to pray, it's just going to happen by them standing up because I am going to prove to you that angels are here. I thought, "That was weird. Was that God or just me?" Then I thought, "I have to go for it because if I don't go for it, I will never know." But, it had been a really good meeting up to that point and worship had been great. The previous night was wonderful. Faith was very high. If I say that and it doesn't happen, it is going to kill this meeting. So wisdom says wait and do it at the very end. That way if you are wrong, it is not going to create too much damage. Then, I immediately had another thought, "No, do it now!" I knew that last one was not my thought because I had already had my good idea. Now listen, when you are not sure it's God you don't have to pretend you do. So, I said, "I think God just told me there are angels here and I think he said he was going to prove it to me because you are going to feel wind hit you or pressure come on your shoulders. When you do, if you will stand up, he will heal you without anybody saying a word. Nobody will pray for you. We are not going to do anything. We are just going to wait and He is going to do it. So if it happens, it was God and if it doesn't, it was me." You may say, "That sure doesn't build much faith." You know what, if it's really God you don't have to pretend your faith is higher than what it is. If it is really the Lord, just say what you think he said and let him prove it. So I said, "I want everybody to be still and do not move or talk or create a false wind or anything. We are just going to wait five minutes starting now." Two of the longest minutes of my life went by without anything happening. In the third minute, people began to stand all over the place. At the end of it, I said, "Five minutes is up. Check your body out. How many of you were healed?" I then said, "If you were healed come down and tell us what you were healed of." Seventy-five people came down and told us of glorious healings. Nobody had said a word. God proved it to me. I was really getting excited.

GOD REINFORCES HIS POINT

Then, I was in Brazil another time in Volta Redonda, the same place where the wind came through. This time my friend, Gary Oates, was taken out of his body into heaven and ultimately saw the Lord. (I won't relate his full story here. You can read it in its entirety in his book, *Open My Eyes, Lord*). When he came back into his body (I saw him come out of the trance into his body again), he was shot backwards and knocked down three rows of chairs and almost knocked a man down in the fourth row. He was this non-mystical type guy lying there weeping. Gary is an organizer and likes to stay in control. However, God just apprehended him. Following that time, he began seeing angels. To this very day, he has this gift that comes every once in awhile and he can see what is happening. Now you may say this is all so subjective. What would make you really believe that what he experienced was real. Well, first of all, it totally freaked him out. He told me, "Randy, I think I may be going crazy. I need somebody to talk to." We were in a meeting in a big church of about 3,000 people, all of a sudden during a drama they were doing while the drums were being played, he saw a bunch of angels come out over the top of the crowd. He said, "They just went above us. I need somebody to talk to." Well, the worship leader was born with Down's syndrome and had been healed at six years old and taken to heaven eight times and could also see in the spirit realm. Afterwards, my friend went up to the worship leader and said, "Davi, when those drums were going did you see anything happen?" Davi said, "Yes, a bunch of angels came out from behind and went over the crowd." My friend looked at me and said, "I'm not crazy. I'm not losing my mind, I am beginning to see."

One night we had gone to Manaus, meeting in a church of about 21,000 at that time but which now has about 60,000 members. The first time we were there, they didn't have any walls because they were building as money was received. They only had pillars, ceiling and concrete. This time when I was ministering for healing and said (I had just heard it thunder), "Oh God, let your river flow and let that river flow through here like in Ezekiel and Revelation and wherever the river touches, heal people." I no more than got that out of my mouth when it started pouring down rain. Then came the wind. I wasn't making connections yet. I still hadn't connected the dots in my mind and the wind blew the rain in the section over on the left side. Do you know who was seated there? That was the deaf section and they were getting sopped with water. In a matter of just a few minutes, we had eight deaf people that began hearing. We had our cameras and were saying which testimony should we get? It was glorious! In one of the videos, you can see that I caught the wind accidentally. The wind went completely over this 10,000 seat sanctuary. The ceiling is thirty or forty feet high and you could see that wind swirl all the way across to the other side. People were getting healed all over the place. Now that hadn't happened when we were previously there. Can you imagine a church that seats 10,000? The wind blew the rain and the mist came in and touched our faces up on the platform. The pastor said, "This has not happened since you guys were here before." As a matter of fact our team got a nickname. You know what our team is called in Manaus, Brazil? We found out on another trip there. They nicknamed the team "Wonder Workers". I like that name! My friend Gary Oates, whose eyes had been opened, was teaching. He had never fallen down while teaching. As he was teaching, I saw his eyes roll up and he fell down. I thought, "He's in trouble. He's on the floor and his mike is still on." I knew God was up to something. Gary's wife had also gotten drunk in the spirit and her eyes were opened too. I said, "Kathy, go get the mike and take over." Kathy got up there and she is very prophetic. What happened was Gary saw a 15 foot angel come right down the middle aisle and it just undid him. Kathy got up and did the most bizarre thing. She grabbed the mike and started prophesying to the wind. I mean she literally prophesied to the wind and the wind started blowing inside the sanctuary The walls were no longer open to the outside because construction had been completed. It blew so hard that it blew the back three rows of chairs over. It came up and we had a huge prop door on the platform about two inches thick and that door was blown open and the wind was not blowing outside the church. Earlier in that series of meetings, we had been doing what we did here every night—you know if you are 80% healed, wave two hands above your head, and we were seeing 500 to 800 a night get healed. That was only about 10% of the crowd of 5,000 to 8,000 a night. The last night we had over 10,000 people. Gary came up because I had been encouraging him to tell me what he was seeing. He said, "Randy, there are some warrior angels in this place tonight." I said, "How do you know they are warrior angels. How do you know these different kinds of angels?" He said, "I know they are warrior angels because they all have swords and are dressed like gladiators." I said, "Where are they?" He said, "They are over there in the balcony on that beam." I said, "What are they doing?" He said, "They are standing there like guards." I said,

"Okay, keep me posted." I feel like a blind man who has a seeing-eye dog sometimes. We were ministering and a little bit later Gary came to me and said, "The warrior angels are on the move." I said, "What are they doing." He said: "They are clearing out the heaven. There are black blotches like demonic stuff and they are literally running away. They have the enemy on the run. Heaven is getting cleared out tonight. Heaven is getting opened tonight." I know some of you reading this must be saying, "This teaching is very weird. He is really off and this is getting kind of far out." You might be asking, "How do you know that was really God?" Well, I think I would have questions if I were you and only hearing somebody's subjective story. I would think this could all be a matter of imagination except for the fruit. That night it wasn't 500 or 800 people that got healed. That night, 9,000 of the 10,000 were waving their hands that they had received a healing in their body. The difference between that night and the other nights was the visitation of the warrior angels that cleared the heavens and gave us the open heaven in a greater way. To me, that is evidence that something was taking place.

By the way one night I felt like the Lord was telling me to teach a sermon I had never taught before. I said, "What?" He gave me a scripture and I asked him to give me more, but that's all I got. I said, "God there are 10,000 people out there and you want me to teach something when I don't know what I'm going to say and all I have is a single scripture. There was only silence. I was warring mentally between going with this sermon I knew versus this text and not having any idea what I was going to say. The pastor was introducing me and I still didn't know which way I was going. Right in the middle of that when I was wondering what I should do, I started forward and then turned around to see who pushed me but nobody was there. Actually, there was somebody there that I couldn't see. Therefore, I went with the text. That was all the encouragement I needed.

REVELATION OF WIND AND FIRE

Let's quote Hebrews 1:7. Speaking of the angels, it says: "He makes his angels winds, his servants flames of fire." That's a quote from Psalm 103:20 and 21 and 104:3 and 4. Say it to yourself again, "He makes his angels winds, his servants flames of fire." Turn to Acts 2:1-4.

> *When the day of Pentecost came, they were all together in one place. *Suddenly a sound like the blowing of a violent wind came

from heaven and filled the whole house where they were sitting. ³They saw what seemed to be tongues of fire that separated and came to rest on each of them. ⁴All of them were filled with the Holy Spirit and began to speak in other tongues as the Spirit of God gave them utterance.

The wind and the fire were more than metaphors or signs of the Holy Spirit. The sign of the Holy Spirit was the languages given. If we really see the scripture through Hebrews 1 and Psalm 103, we understand that on the day of the outpouring of the spirit not only was this new relationship given by grace to the Holy Spirit, but there also was a new relationship given by grace to the hosts of heavens, the angels happening at the same time.

Look at Luke 3:16.

¹⁶John the Baptist answered them all: "I baptize you with water, but one more powerful than I will come, the thongs of whose sandals I am not worthy to untie. He will baptize you with the Holy Spirit and with fire."

Right? Note that it's not "as fire". What about "like fire?" No! It's what? It reads, "and with fire." You know, this is interesting. "And" is a word for something in addition to. "As" and "like" are words of similitude. Such as, "it looked like this." In Greek it is "kai" which is like our "and". Jesus is going to baptize you with the Holy Spirit and He is going to baptize you with fire. We know that in one verse, it says, "He makes his servants flames of fire." Then one of the Baptist scholars wrote me and said, "But in the context there he is only talking about purification." In another letter by email, this Greek scholar said: "I think you are pushing it too far." Then I realized that in one of the greatest stories in the whole Bible about consecration and call to the mission, we read in Isaiah 6: "Who shall go for me and whom shall I send?" I said, "Here am I, send me." That response follows after he said: "I am a man of unclean lips living among a people of unclean lips." God spoke to an angel and said, "Go over to the altar and pick up a coal of fire and bring it and touch his unclean lips." I then realized that scripture teaches that some of the activity of angelic beings is to bring a consecrating affect. The Holy Spirit and the angels do a lot of work in tandem. As a matter of fact in the Bible, God is often seen coming riding upon a white horse and the angels are his entourage (Rev 19).

In Exodus 3:2 (one of the most important things in the whole Bible as far as Old Testament History): "There the angel of the Lord appeared to him in flames of fire from within a bush. Moses saw that though the bush was on fire it did not burn up."

In 2 Kings 2:11 we read; "As they were walking along and talking together, suddenly a chariot of fire and horses of fire appeared and separated the two of them, and Elijah went up to heaven in a whirlwind."

My friends, this is not Dorothy and Toto and a tornado in Kansas. These are angelic hosts that came to usher this great man of God into the presence of God. That's why in Psalm 103, looking back over the Hebrew history, the psalmist understood by the revelation of the Holy Spirit that this fire and this wind were angelic activities sent from God. That's what happened when, in the First Baptist Church at Advance, Missouri, the Holy Spirit fell after some had attended a conference in Southern Illinois. They were singing the Spirit Song by John Wimber in this First Baptist Church when all of a sudden they heard the sound of a mighty rushing wind in the church and everybody in the choir was slain in the spirit. The pastor said, "I was so afraid that I got down and stuck my head under the chair. I was afraid to look at what was going on. I heard shrieks, weeping and laughter. In the next few weeks, we saw almost every miracle recorded in the New Testament take place in our church." As I look at my Bible, I can say, this is not a history book. This is the menu from which you can order. But if you don't know the Bible, you don't know what's right and what's not right to order. This word of God is your menu of the wonderful things the Father has prepared for you because of the dream that was fulfilled in Jesus. In fact, the most common word for God in the Bible is "Lord of Hosts". Tragically in the NIV, it is never translated that way. It is translated the Lord God Almighty because the translators felt that Lord of Hosts didn't make sense. When it is translated Lord of Hosts, we see that He is the Lord over a host of angels fully prepared to do His bidding.

FELLOW SERVANTS

The last thing we will consider is Revelation 19:10. John sees an angel and falls down at the angel's feet. The angel of the Lord says, "Do not do it! I am a fellow servant with you and with your brothers who hold to the testimony of Jesus. Worship God!" First of all, the angel says, I am a fellow servant with you and with your brothers who hold to the testimony of Jesus. Secondly, what I want to emphasize here is that we never worship angels. We need to come to the place of balance as we consider angels. The secular culture really believes in the angelic. It is inside the church that we think they are mythological and legendary and don't have a whole lot of faith in them. Or we feel they are historical but God doesn't do it that way today. I am just trying to say, "Oh, what a great plan of salvation that he would love us so much." Don't worship the angels. May they not be the focus, but may you be aware that you are not alone. There is a heavenly Air Force and we have learned from the earthly wars that whoever controls the air, mops up on the ground. I am so glad our heavenly Air Force has their Air Force outnumbered 2 to 1 because only a third of them was cast out. There are at least two-thirds that remain faithful to the Lord who are fellow servants. I don't know if this makes the spiritual world more real, promises more real and scripture more relevant to today. So, I go back to the question that Omar Cabrera asked me, "Why don't we North Americans ask God to send his angels as well as the Holy Spirit into our meetings?" I didn't tell you this next part because he also said, "The more angels you have in the meeting, the stronger the anointing is in the meeting." Did you ever wonder why it says the angels are ascending and descending? If they have been here working, the anointing is drawn or given away. In a sense the anointing is drained or lost. The level of anointing is decreased in some manner. They are like us and receive anointing from God. They must return to the throne room to receive more anointing from God so they have strength and so that they have anointing to give away. The anointing they carry is not their own; it is from God. We are wired 110 watts and that's why when we get to close to God, we short out. Angels, I believe, are wired 440 watts. That's why they can enter into the throne room and that is also why we must have and will need glorified bodies. I thank God for such a wonderful plan of salvation. I thank Him for the death of Jesus that made it possible. That's my focus and it is He whom we worship.

In this introductory chapter, I have laid a foundation for angelic intervention based on biblical revelation and personal experiences. It is clear to me that we need to understand more of the ways of God so that we may minister healing and deliverance more effectively. The rest of this book will be a closer examination of biblical teaching coupled with personal testimonies of angelic encounters to help build our faith. We will also learn that we can position ourselves to make better connections with the spiritual realm.

CHAPTER 2

WHAT THE BIBLE HAS TO SAY ABOUT ANGELS

Brazil is one of the most on-fire nations to which Global Awakening has been taking teams over many years to experience the more of God. Due to the high level of passion and hunger for God, we get to see Jesus save and heal thousands of people on every trip. The blind see, the deaf hear, the mute speak and the lame walk! We want Christians to be able to experience these types of salvations and miracles to increase their faith to see the Lord do the same manifestations of His glory wherever they live. Many of our team members have also had intense visitations of Heaven and angels due to the extreme openness of Brazil. One of our greatest trips every year is called the Youth Power Invasion. We take a few hundred youth and young adults from America to team up with a few hundred Brazilian youth and young adults. We train and equip them to preach, teach and pray for the sick. Then send them out into churches to do what they just learned.

On one of these trips in Curitiba, Brazil in 2004, a young man named Brandon Hess from Camp Hill, Pennsylvania, was on his first trip to Brazil. He had never experienced miracles before, or the high level of spiritual warfare that can come on ministry trips. Many say that about 8 out of 10 Brazilians at some point in their life have been to a witch doctor for counsel. Brazil is a country very open to spiritism and the occult. Many times, Global teams find themselves engaging in deliverance ministry. Below is the experience he had in Brazil on this trip.

"After a few days of seeing a lot of miracles and healings I came back to my hotel room. As I walked into the room, this fear came over me and I had this gross feeling which I didn't like. But the feeling wasn't attached to a situation, it was attached to a location. Now I was completely new at this, everything spiritual. I was always a Christian, but I did not have a real understanding of the spiritual world. So I was thinking, 'I don't know what that is! I bet a witch did something weird to my room. What do I do? Oh God, I have to sleep in here!'

"So I went next door where I knew a youth pastor was staying. I knocked on his door, and I asked him to come over to my room because it was scary in there. He gave me a really annoyed look and said to his roommate, 'I'll be back (with a negative tone).' The youth pastor grabbed his Bible and sat on my bed. He said, 'What you do when you're afraid is you read Psalm 91 (with a sheepish voice).' I thought, 'Sure! Great, just get the thing out of my room!' The pastor read Psalm 91:1, 'He who dwells in the shelter of the Most High will rest in the shadow of the Almighty.' As he read this verse this peace just came into the room. I thought, 'This is wild!'"

"Then he read it through as I was just sitting on the edge of my bed. He read to verse 12,

> *[11]For he will command his angels concerning you to guard you in all your ways; [12]they will lift you up in their hands, so that you will not strike your foot against a stone. (NIV)"*

"Then I looked in the corner of my bedroom and an angel walked in! I could see the angel clearly as I can see everyone else. This wasn't in my mind, but it literally appeared to me, kind of transparent, but just like I see everyone else. I could kind of see through it. But it just showed up with a BAM! And it was a warrior angel. The angel had the characteristics of a woman, and she was holding her sword and looking at me. This wind came into the room that was blowing her hair back and her garments were moving. There was intense fire in her eyes."

"I was on the edge of my bed while the youth pastor was still reading and at this point I was literally trembling with fear because of the angel and what I was seeing. And he said, 'Brandon, stop (with an annoyed tone). You don't have to be afraid.' I was trembling in my boots! That is why I can picture Jesus telling His angels the first thing to say is, 'Fear not!' This angel was looking at me and it was scary, but at the same time I was feeling, 'You are protected.' That feeling of protection came all around me."

"I told the youth pastor what I was experiencing and he said, 'You mean there is an angel right over there in the corner?' And I said, 'YEAH!' He exclaimed, 'I'm going to tell it to come closer.' And I yelled, 'Oh no, no, don't do that, ahhhh (with a fearful voice)' And I started freaking out! Just then I looked and a white angel walked into the room. The angel just stood there staring at me. Then other angels began to come into the room. I thought, 'What is this?'"

"Then I heard a knock on the door. Randy Clark was at the door looking for his son Josiah. He said, 'Hi Brandon.' And I was still shaking and trembling. He asked, 'What is the matter?' I said trembling, 'Ehh, I just saw an angel!' Randy asked, 'Where?' Randy walked in and I pointed to the corner and he asked, 'In that corner?' I answered, 'Yeah,' as the warrior angel continued looking at me. Randy said, 'Pray for me!' So I prayed, 'Jesus, give it to him! I don't want to be the only weird one seeing this!' Randy responded, 'Brandon, I don't see anything, but I will send Jamie Galloway up.' (Jamie was an intern with Randy who can see in the Spirit realm and has had many credible experiences with angels.)"

"So I was standing in the room thinking, 'Please don't leave! I don't want to be in here alone!' So then a few minutes later Jamie came up to the room.

He said, 'Hey Brandon. So you're seeing?'

I said, 'Yeah....'

Jamie said, 'So you see the blue ones over there?'

And I looked and screamed, 'Ahh! I didn't see those before!'

Jamie said, 'And you see this here?'

I asked, 'What?'

"He said, 'Look. See that man hole?' I saw it as well. Jamie continued, 'That's a portal; watch.' As we watched the portal, it burst into light and water began to come from it. Jamie said, 'If you stand in that, you're going straight to heaven!' So Jamie began to coach me in what we were seeing in the spirit. He started teaching me about what some of the colors meant; like white represents the Word, the purity of God, blue is revelation. Then he stated, 'That angel in the corner is a warrior.'"

"Jamie then left and I was still freaking out about what I was experiencing. Then all of a sudden I felt this cold rush come over me. I looked, and in the spirit it was like circular rivers. If you put your hand in it, it felt like you were in a freezer. A few guys came into my room after all of this. We stayed up till 5:30 A.M. just in the glory, I mean what an experience! So they came in wondering what was happening and the entire night no one saw what I was seeing. The only thing they saw was when there was a gold angel. Where the angel was standing, the footprints were illuminated on the carpet. The carpet just lighted up. Anyone who came in there could have seen the footprints!"

"I looked across the room where my friend Jerrod was. He was on the bed moving his arm and he said, 'Dude, I can't stop moving my hand!' And that made sense as I saw an angel grabbing his wrist and moving it around. You could see a white circle around his wrist as if someone held their fingers around his wrist."

"Then where my friend Billy was standing, there were two angels on either side of him. Billy was in a state of complete peace. He said, 'Dude, I can feel two angels around me.' And I said, 'That's because there are two right there.' Throughout the entire night, what they were feeling I could see. Then my brother was lying on the bed and I saw an angel look over at me and smile. I thought, 'What is he doing?' And the angel went over to my brother and touched his knee. My brother was startled and exclaimed, 'Who touched my knee?' I said, 'That was an angel!'"

"Then there was a guy from Alaska on the trip who we just met, and he called home from the room and was whispering over the phone, 'Hey mom, eh, we're seeing angels.' And you could hear her saying, 'What? (with a disgruntled tone).' He said, 'Yeah, I'm here with…one sec, what are your names again? [Brandon, Billy, etc…] Yeah, it's wild Mom.' It was so new for all of us. We had no box to fit it in. This continued happening and different colored angels continued coming in the room."

"I looked over and the door to the room was cracked open the entire time we were in there. I thought we had woken up the entire nation of Brazil screaming and yelling with the door open. So I went to shut the door, and just as I was about to shut it, the Lord told me, 'Do not shut this door.' So I took a step back and I looked and in the door crack came in a river. It started to pour in through the door. I could see the carpet all of a sudden shimmering with light, as if it was living water. There were sparks coming through it. It was as if the water itself was alive. I saw the water coming through the carpet. Then it touched my feet. And the peace of God literally consumed me like I had never experienced before."

"I began to soak in the river and the river just continued flowing in. I told the guys, 'Hey guys, water is coming in the room." My brother was on the bed and he asked, 'Is the water up to our knees right now?' And I could see that it was. We could literally feel the water level rising in the room of the Lord's peace. I just laid in it thinking how crazy this was. It came to a point where the river was up to our knees, then up to our waist. Then there came a point where I couldn't distinguish what was the ceiling and the level of the river as our room was filled with the Lord's peace. It was wild!"

"Then a guy who had been sleeping on the couch said, 'Hey guys! I smell fruit trees. I smell fruit trees!' And that made sense because I could see a big tree growing in our room and large sized fruit was hanging right over his nose. And I told him what I saw. We were all amazed, and then I put my nose in and began to smell and I could also smell the fruit! My mom opened the door and she was shocked that we were still awake. So we finally went to bed and only got an hour of sleep."

"The next day I went into my mom's room and she asked me what I saw in her room. I actually saw a disgusting looking demon in her room. She was stunned because the night before she could sense an evil presence in her room, but she was afraid to look. So I told the demon to leave and it did. A big muscular looking angel came into the room once the demon left. My mom said she wasn't sure if she would have believed my story if it were someone else besides her son."

"This same day I went to a church service where I was asked to share my experience and share what I was seeing in the church. As I shared this story, a pack of angels came into the sanctuary and stood behind seven individuals. I asked the Lord what they were doing and He said, 'These are the people that I am about to heal. I want you to tell them that.' So I called them all out, and all of them said they were in need of healing. I prayed and asked the Lord to have His angels do whatever they were sent to do. All seven people were healed! So it brought new light to John 5:19 where Jesus said, 'I tell you the truth, the Son can do nothing by himself; he can do only what he sees his Father doing.' So if we can see what God is doing, we can move right with Heaven and have success." (B. Hess 2008)

Now four years later, Brandon still can see angels wherever he goes. He has many testimonies of seeing angels on his college campus, Penn State, and co-laboring with them to bring healing and salvation. He is just one of many people who have been powerfully touched on one of our trips and launched into a new level of anointing. What was amazing about Brandon's experience was that he actually experienced what we read about in Ezekiel 47:1-7; 12 and he didn't even know it!

¹The man brought me back to the entrance of the temple, and I saw water coming out from under the threshold of the temple toward the east (for the temple faced east). The water was coming down from under the south side of the temple, south of the altar. ²He then brought me out through the north gate and led me around the outside to the outer gate facing east, and the water was flowing from the south side.

³As the man went eastward with a measuring line in his hand, he measured off a thousand cubits and then led me through water that was ankle-deep. ⁴He measured off another thousand cubits and led me through water that was knee-deep. He measured off another thousand and led me through water that was up to the waist. ⁵He measured off another thousand, but now it was a river that I could not cross, because the water had risen and was deep enough to swim in—a river that no one could cross. ⁶He asked me, "Son of man, do you see this?" Then he led me back to the bank of the river. ⁷When I arrived there, I saw a great number of trees on each side of the river.

¹² [The Lord said] "Fruit trees of all kinds will grow on both banks of the river. Their leaves will not wither, nor will their fruit fail. Every month they will bear, because the water from the sanctuary flows to them. Their fruit will serve for food and their leaves for healing." (NIV)

The purpose of this chapter is to lay a Biblical foundation of what the Bible has to say about angels. We don't want to read the Bible only for historical purposes and to have only head knowledge about angels. We want to read these stories of how God sent angels to normal men and women like you and me. We want to see them as open invitations for God to do the same thing with us as He did with them. Brandon's story is a great example because Brandon experienced something similar to what Ezekiel experienced thousands of years ago! So with this attitude and outlook upon the Scriptures, let's see what the Bible has to say about ANGELS!

WHAT ARE ANGELS?

In the Bible, our English word "angel" is translated from the Hebrew word *mal'āk* 112 times in the Old Testament, and the Greek word *angelos* 167 times in the New Testament. However, a few times in the Old and New Testament there were angelic visitations, but the author did not use the word 'angel' to describe their experience. Ezekiel wrote that he had many visitations with heavenly beings, but the word "angel" was never used. Similarly, Daniel in his series of visions in Daniel 7, 8 and 10 never uses the word angel, yet the angel we know as Gabriel is mentioned. The other "figures" were described as "ones who looked like men." Acts 1:10 describes two men in white robes who were at the ascension of Jesus Christ. Another example is when Jacob wrestled with a man in Genesis 32:34. We know this was an angel from Hosea 12:4 where it says,

4He [Jacob] struggled with the angel and overcame him;
he wept and begged for his favor. He found him at Bethel
and talked with him there. (NIV)

It is very important to understand what an angel is. Angels were created by God (Col. 1:16), and are spiritual beings, meaning they are spirits without a human body. J. Rodman Williams has a very insightful perspective on angels. In his book, *Renewal Theology*, he writes:

> "Angels are pure spiritual beings. In the Book of Hebrews angels are described as 'ministering spirits' (1:14). The word for 'spirits' is *pneumata*, the plural form of *pneuma* ('spirit'), which is also used in relation to God, for example, in John 4:24—'God is spirit.'" (J. Williams 1998: 173)

Since angels are spirits, we understand that they are a part of the unseen realm/ invisible world that the Bible talks about. Many in these days would also term this the 'spirit realm.' John used this terminology as well in Revelation 1:10 where he says, "I was in the Spirit." He goes on to write about seeing or hearing myriads of angels. John uses the word 'angel' almost 70 times in his writings! That is almost 40% of the times the word angel is used in the New Testament.

Because angels are created by God, we know that they are not omnipresent like God. They are not as powerful or authoritative as God. Theologians differ on when angels were created, and actually most discussions result from differing understandings of when Satan fell from heaven. Some believe angels were created before the heavens and the earth were created in Gen. 1:1. This conclusion comes from Job 38:4-7 where "sons of God" is used referring to angels. This means that when God laid the foundation of the earth, the angels were rejoicing which implies that they were already created. Others believe angels were created after the 7 days of creation. This is due to Scriptures that refer to the fall of Lucifer along with a third of the angels (Is. 14:12; Luke 10:18; Rev. 12:9). Lucifer, Satan or the devil (whichever you prefer to call him) was originally created a good angel because God can only create out of Himself, and no part of Him is evil, but only good. Their viewpoint is Lucifer had to have fallen after the seven days of creation because the Bible says that God looked at all that He had made and called it "very good" in Gen. 1:31.

Others believe that when Gen. 1:2 says, "The earth was formless and void, and darkness was over the surface of the deep," that darkness means Satan and the fallen angels had already been thrown to earth at this point and were occupying earth. It is interesting that Genesis 2:1 says, "Thus the heavens and the earth were completed, and all their hosts." The word "hosts" means an army, or a large assembly of created beings! All of this to say, there is no clear position based upon Scripture when angels were created. We do know that Satan shows up in Genesis 3, meaning at that point angels had been created, and some had fallen.

FUNCTIONS OF ANGELS

The word angel means a messenger. In their original nature, angels were created to give messages to mankind from the Lord. We see that throughout the Bible angels gave messages to Hagar (Gen. 16), Abraham (Gen.18), Moses (Exodus 3:2), Mary, mother of Jesus (Luke 1:26), Joseph (Matt. 1:20-24), Paul (Acts 27:23) and John (Rev 1:1) to name a few. Another duty that angels are assigned to do is perform God's word.

Psalm 103:20

> ^{20}Bless the LORD, you His angels,
> who excel in strength, who do His word,
> heeding the voice of His word. (NKJV)

This means that whatever God says, angels are commissioned to ensure that what God has spoken comes to pass. Every prophetic word then has an angelic assignment. Every time the Lord says there will be healing, an angel is assigned to make that healing occur. When the Lord says to protect a person, an angel is assigned to protect that individual.

Another function of an angel is to minister to the heirs of salvation (Heb. 1:14). What does minister mean? Minister means to serve. Angels ministered to Jesus after he was tempted (Matt. 4:11; Mark 1:13) and also before his crucifixion in Gethsemane (Luke 22:43). If Jesus of all people needed angels to minister to him, how much more do we need angels to minister to us! More important than angels, we need more of Jesus. That is why Hebrews 4:16 is such an incredible verse for believers in Jesus Christ; *Let us therefore come boldly to the throne of grace, that we may obtain mercy and find grace to help in time of need* (NKJV). Sometimes, whether we know it or not, the Lord will send His angels to minister to us. An angel strengthened Daniel during an encounter (Dan. 10:18). If angels could strengthen people in the Old Testament times, then they can strengthen those who are heirs of salvation in the New Testament era.

Philippians 4:13

[13] I can do all things through Christ who strengthens me. (NKJV)

Although angels are assigned to serve those who are believers in Jesus Christ, they are assigned a higher purpose: to worship God! James Goll in his book, <u>Angelic Encounters</u>, writes, "Angels give service to God—worshipping God eternally (See Psalm 148:2)." (J. Goll 2007: 67). Also, the Bible tells us this in the Apostle John's revelation of the throne room in Rev. 4 and 5 where he saw large numbers of angels and heavenly creatures worshipping the Lord. Isaiah 6 describes some of the heavenly beings crying out, "Holy, Holy, Holy" day and night worshipping God.

Terry Law is the author of <u>The Truth About Angels</u>, one of the best foundational books on angels. In this book, he has some tremendous insights on the function of angels. He writes concerning the duties angels had in revealing the Ten Commandments and the writing of the law:

> *"Angels had something to do with giving Israel the law through Moses. This is recorded in the New Testament where Stephen said in his great speech before the high priest that Israel had 'received the law by the disposition of angels, and have not kept it.' (Acts 7:53). Paul also said the law was 'ordained by angels'" (Gal. 3:19). (T. Law 1994: 85)*

Law also explains that according to Luke 16:22, angels have an assignment in transporting individual's spirits after they die to heaven or to hell. This would explain why there are many stories of people right before they die who begin to experience seeing angels in their room, or seeing a light. (T. Law 1994: 118) Stephen had this experience as well before he was stoned in Acts 7:55-56.

CHARACTERISTICS OF ANGELS

Angels exhibit many unusual characteristics worthy of examination. One is that angels can have their own language. Paul writes in 1 Corinthians 13:1 that it is possible to speak in the tongues of angels. James Goll writes concerning other characteristics of angels,

> "They [angels] are personal beings, and they possess:

- A personal will (1 Peter 1:12)
- Intelligent minds (2 Sam. 14:17, 20)
- Emotional responses, such as joy (Heb. 12:22; Luke 15:10) and contentiousness (Jude 9; Rev. 12:7)" (J. Goll 2007: 41)

We know angels have a will because Lucifer had an opportunity to rebel against God. This means angels are not robots, and therefore have a choice to make whether or not they obey God just as humans do. However, angels do not have the opportunity to receive salvation. Jesus did not die for angels to be saved, or Lucifer and the fallen angels would have the opportunity to repent. Only mankind has the opportunity to repent, which angels cannot experience, therefore longing to understand what salvation is like!

> "—They [angels] want to understand redemption (1 Pet. 1:12). –They observe the affairs of the redeemed (1 Cor. 4:9; 11:10; 1 Tim. 5:21). –They are to gain a better understanding of God's wisdom as it is displayed through the church (Eph. 3:9-10). – They know when the lost become 'found' by God and rejoice over their salvation (Luke 15:10). –They apparently stay busy ministering to people in various ways, yet we do not have to do anything for angels." (T. Law 1994: 109)

Some other interesting facts about angels are: some have swords (Num. 22:22, 1 Chron. 21:27); they do not marry or die (Luke 20:35-36); and some are assigned to execute the righteous judgment of God (see 2 Sam. 24:16-17 where 70,000 people were killed and 2 Kings 19:35 where 185,000 were killed). The Bible says that angels will not die, but the Scriptures are silent about whether God does or does not create more angels. Humans are still being created every day, as well as natural phenomena. New clouds spring up everyday, as well as trees, plants, fruits and animals as well. So we know the nature of God as Creator is to create all the time. He is still creating new stars and galaxies (proven by science), so is it possible that He is still creating new angels? Scripture is not clear on this issue, but if we know that Satan fell and took a third of the angels, then that might imply that there are a fixed number of angels when God created them. Or it could simply be that a third of the angels which existed at that time were the ones that fell.

Due to the mystery of the number of angels, we have to rely on what the Bible says concerning how many angels actually exist. Daniel 7:10 says:

[10] A river of fire was flowing,
coming out from before him.
Thousands upon thousands attended him;
ten thousand times ten thousand stood before him.
The court was seated,
and the books were opened. (NIV)

Ten thousand times ten thousand equals one hundred million angels. Jesus says in Matthew 25:53 about the ability for twelve legions (3,000 – 6,000) of angels to be sent to him by the Father. In John's revelation of Jesus, he writes that there were myriads and thousands of angels. And none of these numbers may actually represent the total of all angels.

Revelation 5:11

[11] Then I looked, and I heard around the throne and the living creatures and the elders the voice of many angels, numbering myriads of myriads and thousands of thousands. (ESV)

Myriads comes from the Greek word *murias* which means ten thousand times ten thousand, innumerable multitude or an unlimited number. This is the same phrase Daniel used to describe what he was experiencing. There were just too many to count! That is a lot of angels worshipping God. This number doesn't even include the angels that were on the earth on assignment. We have a lot of very awesome teammates and fellow fighters, servants and ministers on our side (Job 25:3; Heb. 12:22)! Like Elisha described the army of the Lord in 2 Kings 6:16, "[16]Do not fear, for those who are with us are more than those who are with them." The enemy has nothing compared to the army of angels and hosts that are on the side of believers in Jesus Christ."

GUARDIAN ANGELS

There are many different beliefs concerning guarding angels, especially as the New Age movement has matured and increased over the past decades and more and more people have been drawn into deception. The Bible does, however, give us some answers about guardian angels.

Matthew 18:10

> *[Jesus said] See that you do not look down on one of these little ones. For I tell you that their angels in heaven always see the face of my Father in heaven." (NIV)*

Psalm 34:7

> *The angel of the LORD encamps around those who fear him, and he delivers them. (NIV)*

Psalm 91:11

> *For he will command his angels concerning you to guard you in all your ways. (NIV)*

Another place the Bible suggests that angels are assigned to people is in Acts 12 when Peter is rescued from prison by an angel. The church was praying for him to be freed from prison, and the Lord answered their prayers. Peter knocked on the door of the praying believers, but they did not believe it was him, but his angel. Now, I'm not sure about you, but if an angel was at my door, I would be there in a heartbeat to welcome the angel in! In this case, however, the angel appeared to look like Peter, so maybe Rhoda was too stunned to open the door.

Revelation 22:16

> *"I, Jesus, have sent My angel to testify to you these things for the churches..." (NASB)*

This verse indicates that even Jesus has a personal angel. So if Peter had an angel that looked like him, and Jesus says "My angel" then we can surmise that we also have an angel and even one that could very well look like us! If the people in Acts 12 thought that it was Peter's angel that means that an angel looked like him to the point of being mistaken as Peter.

FALLEN ANGELS AND ANGELS OF DECEPTION

We previously looked at the fall of Satan from heaven along with a third of the angels (Is. 14:12; Luke 10:18; Rev. 12:9). This part of the chapter is not intended to give any credit to Satan, or to focus our attention on him or his fallen angels that are under his authority. However, we are in a war between the kingdom of darkness and the kingdom of light. It is wise to be knowledgeable about your opponent or your enemy. Therefore this section's purpose is to make the reader aware of the reality of fallen angels. (See Chapter 3 on becoming equipped to discern between Godly angels and fallen angels.)

"The Bible warns against receiving false doctrine from supposed angels: 'But even if we, or an angel from heaven, should preach to you a gospel contrary to that which we preached to you, let him be accursed' (Gal. 1:8). Paul makes this warning because he knows that there is a possibility of deception. He says, "Even Satan disguises himself as an angel of light' (2 Cor. 11:14)." (W. Grudem 1994: 406)

The letters of Paul, John and Peter are very clear in their warnings about false doctrines, false prophets, false apostles, false worship and the antichrist spirit. Since there can be a false source, that means there is a true source, Jesus Christ. We do need to be aware of what is false so that we can lead people in the truth. It would have been careless for Paul, Peter and John to write under their apostolic authority and not warn the sheep of the wolves and the false doctrines and predators that were around to devour them. In saying this we should always remember not to fear the enemy or his agents called demons, evil spirits or fallen angels. They have been soundly defeated by Jesus through his death and resurrection (Colossians 2:15).

Colossians 2:11-15

[11]In him also you were circumcised with a circumcision made without hands, by putting off the body of the flesh, by the circumcision of Christ, [12]having been buried with him in baptism, in which you were also raised with him through faith in the powerful working of God, who raised him from the dead. [13]And you, who were dead in your trespasses and the uncircumcision of your flesh, God made alive together with him, having forgiven us all our trespasses, [14]by canceling the record of debt that stood against us with its legal demands. This he set aside, nailing it to the cross. [15]He disarmed the rulers and authorities and put them

to open shame, by triumphing over them in him. (ESV)

1 Corinthians 15:57

[57]But thanks be to God, who gives us the victory through our Lord Jesus Christ. (ESV)

1 John 5:4

[4]For everyone who has been born of God overcomes the world. And this is the victory that has overcome the world—our faith. (ESV)

As we can see, the saints of the kingdom of God have the victory through the blood of Jesus Christ. The reason we need to be aware of angels of darkness is their ability to pose as angels of light. Fallen angels influenced the 1st century church, and they have been doing it ever since, right up to today. When people have believed some of these dark angels of light, it has resulted in the formation of some of the world's leading cults and false religions. Two of them are Islam and Mormonism. Below are excerpts from Terry Law's research on these two religions.

"While meditating in a cave, Mohammed began to have violent seizures and frightening visions, allegedly from the angel Gabriel. His first thought was that these were demonic, but his wife persuaded him that they were divine and that he should listen to 'the angel.' Out of these revelations, which lasted twenty-two years until his death in A.D. 632 at about sixty-four years of age, came the youngest major world religion – Islam." (T. Law 1994: 49)

"An angel of light (or angels of light) appeared to Joseph Smith in similar fashion as with Mohammed. Three years later another angel – or the same one in another guise – appeared calling himself Moroni. At times Smith said the angel's name was Nephi." (T. Law 1994: 51)

"Parallel strands of doctrines run through [both] these religions. The same strands are in mythologies, Gnosticism and so forth, and are distortions or perversions of basic Judeo-Christian truths." (T. Law 1994: 51-52)

Islam is now the 2nd largest religion in the world behind Christianity. The entire religion is based upon an encounter with a false angel of light! This religion is also extremely violent against the belief systems of Christianity. It is very interesting that Paul and John were battling the same demonic forces of Gnosticism in the 1st century as we are today in the 21st century. This is why we need to be careful concerning modern day angelic encounters. We should not be fearful of them or skeptical of them, but careful and discerning according to the Word of God.

DO NOT WORSHIP ANGELS

The Bible clearly states that we are to worship God only and no other person, spirit, or thing (Ex. 20:5; Col. 2:18). If we do, then we are practicing idolatry and sin. One of the best ways to know if an angel is from God is based upon whether or not they allow you to worship them. Angels come from the very throne of God where His glory is. They enter into the earth realm carrying His glory. This can make it extremely hard for man because we are attracted to that glory and begin to worship the being instead of God. Even the apostle John began to worship the angel in Revelation 19:10. The angel stopped him and told him that he was a fellow servant and to worship God only. Bill Johnson has a great quote concerning angels. He says, "While it is foolish to worship angels, it is equally foolish to ignore them." (J. Goll 2007: Foreword)

In the same manner we are not to pray to angels or even saints as some Christians and other religions believe. Here is what Wayne Grudem says at this point:

> "Nor should we pray to angels. We are to pray only to God, who alone is omnipotent and thus able to answer prayer and who alone is omniscient and therefore able to hear the prayers of all his people at once. By virtue of omnipotence and omniscience, God the Son and God the Holy Spirit are also worthy of being prayed to, but this is not true of any other being. Paul warns us against thinking that any other mediator can come between us and God, 'for there is one God, and there is *one mediator* between God and men, the man Christ Jesus' (1 Tim. 2:5). If we were to pray to angels, it would be implicitly attributing to them a status equal to God, which we must not do." (W. Grudem 1994: 407)

WHAT SHOULD BE THE EXPECTATION OF ANGELIC ENCOUNTERS TODAY?

As we have seen, the Bible has a lot to say about angels. God sent angels to his people throughout Scripture, from Genesis to Revelation. There were multiple angelic encounters in the Old and New Testament. Many of the people to whom God sent angels were ordinary people. Many of the saints had no idea what to do with the experiences except obey and believe the word of the Lord.

Here are some examples of angelic encounters in the Bible. Hagar, the mother of Ishmael, encountered the angel of the Lord in Genesis 16:7-11 and Genesis 21:17; Abraham did as well in Genesis 18 and 22 when he was about to kill his son Isaac. In Genesis 19, Lot encountered two angels before the destruction of Sodom and Gomorrah. Jacob encountered angels in a dream in Genesis 28:12 and Genesis 31:1. Angels met him in 32:1 and he wrestled with one in 32:34 who changed his identity and name to Israel. Moses encountered an angel that manifested as a burning bush in Exodus 3:2. The angel of the Lord was with Moses and the Israelites in Exodus 14:19; 23:20, 23 and 32:34. In chapter 33, the Lord was upset with His people and told Moses that He was no longer going with them, but He would send His angel before them. Angels are awesome. Angelic protection would have been sufficient, but Moses wanted more than just an angel, he wanted only God! Because of Moses' desire for the presence of God, the Lord decided to stay with Moses and Israel. We should be like Moses in the fact that we accept angels and are happy to receive their counsel, guidance and strength, but our focus should always be Jesus Christ and we should desire Him above any other encounter or experience!

Joshua saw the captain of the Lord's army in Joshua 5:15. Gideon had a powerful encounter with an angel in Judges 6:11-22. The mother and father of Samson had an angel sent to them in Judges 13. David saw an angel of destruction in 2 Samuel 24:16-17 and retold in 1 Chronicles 2. An angel appeared to Elijah to strengthen him and gave him food to eat in 1 Kings 19:5-7 and an angel spoke to him in 2 Kings 1:15. Elisha saw a chariot of fire as Elijah was taken up to heaven in 2 Kings 2:11. Elisha again saw chariots in 2 Kings 6:17. Shadrach, Meshach and Abednego were saved from death by an angel in Daniel 3. Daniel was also saved by an angel in the lion's den in Daniel 6:22. Daniel had many other visitations with angels including the angel Gabriel, and was told about the angel Michael (Daniel 7-12). Zechariah also had some extreme visions and experiences with angels. Most of the book of Zechariah consists of his experience with the angels and the visions.

In the New Testament, Gabriel shows up again, appearing to the father of John the Baptist, Zacharias in Luke 1:11-19. Then to Mary the mother of Jesus in Luke 1:26-38 and to Joseph in Matthew 1:20-24. An angel appears to Joseph on two more occasions in dreams in Matthew 2:13 and 2:19. As mentioned before, angels ministered to Jesus in Matthew 4:11, Mark 1:13, and Luke 22:43. As stated in chapter 1, Jesus very likely had more encounters with angels. We conclude this from his statement in John 1:51, about angels ascending and descending upon him. Angels appeared at the tomb of Jesus' resurrection in Matthew 28:5; Luke 22:43; John 20:12. Two men appeared at the ascension of Jesus in Acts 1:10. An angel rescued the apostles from prison in Acts 5:19 and again Peter in Acts 12:7-10. Paul had an experience with an angel in Acts 27:23, and in 2 Corinthians 12 Paul describes how some of his heavenly experiences and visions were so amazing that he could not tell anyone. John had a very long visitation with many angels and Jesus Christ in the book of Revelation. Also, in many of these accounts the angels and individuals had a conversation back and forth, meaning that we as humans can communicate with angels when initiated by them.

It appears that both Paul and John were familiar with the Spirit realm. The Bible does not give more details about more encounters, but in my opinion, we might assume that they did. Even in John 21:25, Johns writes that Jesus performed numerous miracles and preached many messages in three years of ministry that not even the world could contain all the written accounts of what he did. Jesus admitted in John 3:13 that he had been to heaven since being on the earth. John and Paul had more than three years of ministry, and again we might assume they had more experiences with angels, Jesus, heaven, visions, trances, healings, miracles, signs and wonders than are recorded. As they grew in love, in character and spread the Gospel, they also had these types of supernatural experiences. They wrote about them in the epistles, showing that all of these types of fruit are part of the normal Christian life. Every experience they had pointed to the one who allowed and initiated the encounter, Jesus Christ. If someone begins to boast about their experiences with angels or heaven or even Jesus, you know that this does not line up with the Word of God, as Jesus is the only one who receives all glory and honor and praise.

Another Biblical account of an angelic encounter to consider is that of Balaam who was a false prophet (Num. 22-35). Shepherds experienced angels in Luke 2:9-15 and went to worship at the birth of Jesus. Cornelius was an unsaved Gentile from Italy who was in the army and had a vision, and in the vision an angel spoke to him (Acts 10:3-7). If you are not of Jewish descent, then you should be thankful that God released an angel to Cornelius. It was an angelic visitation that made the Apostles aware that non-Jewish people could be saved and included in God's family. This opened the door for every person in the world, whether Jew or Gentile to experience salvation as Peter came to the home of Cornelius and his whole family received salvation, were baptized and filled with the Holy Spirit. So unbelievers can have true angelic encounters that should point them to JESUS!!

What is the importance of looking at all these Biblical experiences with angels? In Bill Johnson's message on *The Power of the Testimony*, he speaks of our inheritance as saints. In Psalm 119:111 it says, *"[111]I have inherited Your testimonies forever, for they are the joy of my heart" (NASB)*. These Biblical accounts are our testimonies of God's interaction with mankind. The Bible also describes the incredible power that is released when a testimony is shared. Rev. 19:10 says, *"The testimony of Jesus is the spirit of prophecy" (NASB)*. When we share a testimony of God's goodness or something that He has done, it prophesies that God is willing to do the same thing again, as He is no respecter of persons (Rom. 2:11 KJV). He is the same yesterday, today and forever (Heb. 13:8) What God has done in the past, He is willing to do again because what He has done testifies of His nature. His nature is to visit and communicate with His people. His nature is sometimes to send angels to visit His people because He loves them. Jesus said that every born again Christian is greater in the Kingdom of heaven than everyone in the Old Testament (Matt. 11:11) because they have the Father, the Son and Holy Spirit living in them. That means all of the men and women who encountered God, heaven, angels, miracles, healings, signs and wonders in the Old Testament serve as a revelation of our inheritance as children of God and God wants to do it again in our day and in our lives.

Some Christians believe supernatural phenomena stopped after the last apostle died because they had established the church and the writings of the Scriptures. This theology has been termed cessationism and dispensationalism. Contrary to their thinking, nowhere in the Bible does it say God has stopped talking to His people, stopped bringing people to salvation or performing healings, deliverances, signs, wonders and miracles. All Christians profess to be saved, but most do not understand the full meaning of our English word saved. The original Greek word from which we get "saved" is the word *sozo*. This Greek word means more than just saved, but also healed (Matt. 9:22), delivered (Luke 8:36), restored and preserved. This means salvation in its fullest sense doesn't just mean saved from Hell or from the penalty for our sins, but salvation has a much deeper meaning, restoring the whole person and bringing them fullness of life (John 10:10) and renewed relationship with God. So if one does not believe in healings, miracles, and casting out of demons, then they are technically denying the fullness of salvation that Jesus established through His death and resurrection.

Many people in our day believe that any type of supernatural experience, like an angelic visitation, is false because it is extra-biblical. This means that since the canonization of the Bible, supernatural phenomena ceased to exist because people now have the Bible, even though Hebrews 13:2 exhorts us to be aware that we might entertain angels. Terry Law has this to say about encounters outside of Scripture:

"There is an ocean of difference between that which is 'extra-biblical' and that which is 'unbiblical.' Extra-biblical is a yellow light that encourages passage with caution; unbiblical is a red light that requires travelers to halt in the name of the law and common sense." (T. Law 1994: 55)

People who have an anti-supernatural or anti-charismatic perspective due to a cessationist or dispensationalist viewpoint have missed a huge point in that Paul was not a part of the original twelve apostles. So if there was an 'extra' apostle, then isn't it possible for God to raise up more than one and why wouldn't He? Actually God did raise up more apostles and prophets in the New Testament besides Paul if you search the book of Acts and the writings of Paul. There are Stephen and Philip, who began as servants to the Apostles. Then after years of maturity and sitting under the Apostles' teachings, they were commissioned as Evangelists to share the Gospel. Acts 7 and 8 record their interactions and preaching. Notice that they performed miracles, signs and wonders and both Stephen and Philip encountered an angel! These men were not a part of the original twelve apostles. This means that the original twelve and Paul potentially raised up hundreds if not thousands of people who could operate in the supernatural power of God and who were accustomed to angelic beings (Acts 8:26; 12), and they continued to disciple others and raise them up in the teachings of Jesus Christ. God forgive the church for ever believing that He stopped performing His Word, stopped speaking, stopped healing, stopped prophesying and stopped revealing Himself to His people.

"There seems, therefore, no compelling reason to rule out the possibility of angelic appearances today. Some would dispute this on grounds that the sufficiency of Scripture (see Chapter 8) and the closing of its canon (see Chapter 3) rule out the possibility of angelic manifestations now. They would say that we are not to expect God to communicate to us through angels. However, this conclusion does not follow. Though angels would not add to the doctrinal and moral content of Scripture, God could communicate information to us through angels as he also does through prophecy or through ordinary communication from other persons (like preaching), or through our observation of the world. If God can send another human being to warn us of danger or encourage us when we are downcast, there seems no inherent reason why he could not occasionally send an angel to do this as well." (W. Grudem 1994: 408)

"The biblical evidence demonstrates, then, that we, as God's people, can still talk to and listen to the angelic fellow servants of God's household, as long as our heart still belongs to our Father—as long as our dependence, our devotion and our primary attention is on our Father, Jesus, and the Holy Spirit." (G. Greig 2008: 22)

REASONS WHY THE CHURCH NEEDS TO BE AWARE OF ANGELS

In the 1990's, *Time* wrote an article concerning the growing fascination with angels. Here are a couple of interesting statistics that they found:

"*Time* magazine found that 69 percent of those they polled believe in the existence of angels, and 46 percent believe they have a guardian angel." (T. Law 1994: 19)

"A *Time* poll showed that 49 percent of Americans believe that evil angels exist." (T. Law 1994: 122)

Many children talk about having imaginary friends, or seeing people or monsters in their bedrooms. Is it possible that because of their childlike faith that they are not just imagining these identities, but are actually encountering angels and demons? Have we, as parents undermined our children's faith and ability to see in the spirit realm by convincing them that they are just making up these "imaginary" friends? Jesus said, "In order to see the kingdom, you must become like a little child."

If one watches television, you will find dozens of movies and programs incorporating supernatural phenomena, super heroes and an awareness of the spiritual realm revolving around new age or occult beliefs. These movements have been gradually increasing over the years and the church is beginning to face some of the most intense battles spiritually in its history. It is time for the body of Christ to mature and take their rightful inheritance as children of God. The children of God need an awareness that the most supernatural being, GOD, lives inside of them and the same spirit that raised Jesus Christ from the dead, the Holy Spirit, also lives in them. We need to understand the GODLY Spiritual realm and His supernatural experiences in order to be able to have the Mt. Carmel (1 Kings 18) experiences with the powers of darkness in our age. Instead, the church has cowered in fear and skepticism. We have failed to realize that the Bible is full of experiences with God that are still available to us today in order to fulfill the mandate of the Great Commission that all people would come to salvation (2 Peter 3:9).

If you have been afraid of the supernatural, that is okay. It can be frightening, especially with so much deception. But that does not mean we throw out the foundational truth of the Word of God. Jesus said to follow him in every aspect, Then Paul wrote that we should follow him as he followed Christ (2 Tim. 1:13; 3:10). Since both of these men had supernatural encounters with angels, heaven, miracles, raising of the dead, healings, signs and wonders, love, faith, hope, joy, kindness, etc… how much more should we follow them in all these characteristics of the Christian faith? How much more do we need supernatural experiences to help sustain us and mature us. Paul writes in 1 Cor. 2:14 that things that are spiritual have to be discerned spiritually, not with head knowledge or at face value. He says later in 3:1 that he could only talk to the Corinthian church about basic concepts as they were acting like 'mere men' or 'carnal.' How would Paul write to the body of Christ today concerning spiritual matters? My prayer is that we as the body will grow in our maturity, that we can move from spiritual milk to the meat of God's plans and purposes.

THE AWARENESS OF THE UNSEEN REALM

"Just as the Sadducees in Jesus' day said that 'there is no resurrection, nor angel, nor spirit' (Acts 23:8). So many in our day deny the reality of anything they cannot see. But the biblical teaching on the existence of angels is a constant reminder to us that there is an unseen world that is very real." (W. Grudem 1994: 403)

Paul exhorts us in 2 Corinthians 4:18 to *fix our eyes not on what is seen, but on what is unseen. For what is seen is temporary, but what is unseen is eternal.* (NIV) Colossians 1:15 says that God is invisible and in verse 16 that all things, whether visible or invisible were created by Him and for Him. So we fix our eyes upon Jesus, the Author and Finisher of our faith in all matters. We also need to understand that we are citizens and ambassadors of an unseen world (Eph. 2:19; Phil. 3:20; 2 Cor. 5:20), heaven. Eph. 3:2 says we are seated in heavenly places with Christ Jesus. We are also hidden with Christ (Col. 3:3). We know from John 1:51 that angels ascended and descended on Jesus. Where is Jesus? Jesus is in Heaven at the seated at the right hand of the Father, but He is also in the heart of every born again Christian. This means that we have an open heaven over our lives where the angels of heaven have access to ascend and descend! What do I mean by open heaven? Jesus made a statement that was in reference to an encounter Jacob had in Gen. 28:12-17. Jacob had a dream where he saw a ladder set up on the earth reaching heaven with angels ascending and descending. Jesus was declaring that He was the ladder connecting heaven and earth (Eph. 1:10), which Jacob described as the gate of heaven in verse 17. Since Jesus died on the cross, rose from the dead and ascended into heaven He established a permanent opening from the Earth into the Heavens. Because Jesus had this opening over His life, He carries that over to us. He lives in us and connects us with the world where He dwells now which is HEAVEN! This also means that as believers we have the authority in Christ because we abide in Him. This enables us to release the attributes of the invisible spirit realm into the natural realm. This invisible realm is also called the kingdom of God, or the kingdom of Heaven.

In the gospels, the word "kingdom" is used over 100 times. The kingdom of God was the central message that Jesus taught while on the earth.

Matthew 4:17

17From that time Jesus began to preach and to say, "Repent, for the kingdom of heaven is at hand." (NKJV)

people think that repentance means to kneel at the altar and
heir sins. While there is truth in this concept, there is a
...ing to repentance. The true meaning, according to Greek, is
...ge the way you think." This is explained through a revolutionary
...cept that Bill Johnson writes about in his book, *When Heaven Invades Earth.*

"If the Kingdom is *here and now*, then we must acknowledge
it's in the invisible realm. Yet being *at hand* reminds us that it's
also *within reach*...Jesus told Nicodemus that he'd have to be
born again to *see* the Kingdom [John 3:3]. That which is unseen
can be realized only through *repentance*. It was as though He
said, 'If you don't change the way you perceive things, you'll live
your whole life thinking that what you see in the natural is the
superior reality. Without changing the way you think you'll never
see the world that is right in front of you. It's My world, and it
fulfills every dream you've ever had. And I brought it with Me.'
All that He did in life and ministry, He did by drawing from that
superior reality." (B. Johnson 2003: 38)

Jesus goes on to tell us that the Kingdom of Heaven is within every
believer (Luke 17:21). When we become born again, the Holy Spirit
comes into our spirits, opens the way into the invisible Kingdom of God.
That gives us access to every aspect of who God is, where He is and what
He has stored up for us. We know this because "kingdom" means the
King's domain. God is our King and His domain is Heaven and this is
where He has set up his throne. By the statement Jesus made in Luke 17,
He was declaring that the domain in which the Father lives is accessible
by the Holy Spirit who was about to inhabit all believers. That is why the
apostle John was able to write in Revelation that he was "in the Spirit"
and subsequently saw the very throne of God. John had access to this
realm of Heaven by faith, just as every believer today does because Jesus
told us we could.

Jesus even commands us to seek His Kingdom first (Matt. 6:33).
Jesus taught His disciples to pray for God's kingdom to come on earth as
it is in heaven (Luke 11:2). It is the will of God for His realm to invade
our realm. If you have ever prayed this prayer in Luke 11, then you
have asked God's realm, heaven, to come into the natural realm on earth
whether you knew it or not.

"When we pray for His Kingdom to come, we are asking Him to superimpose the rules, order, and benefits of His world over this one until this one looks like His. That's what happens when the sick are healed or the demonized are set free. His world collides with the world of darkness, and His world always wins." (B. Johnson 2003: 63)

We established earlier that there are so many angels in heaven worshipping God that one cannot count all of them. When we pray for God's kingdom to come to earth, we are not only inviting the fullness of God and His nature and character, we are inviting the entirety of His domain and all of heaven. This means we are inviting the angels that are in heaven and around His throne to come into our natural realm. The more we pray this prayer and the more we expect God's kingdom to invade earth, the more we need to expect and anticipate God showing up and His angels coming with Him. We should not be surprised when angels appear because we are asking for God's will to be done, and angels perform His will (Psalm 103:20). Since there is no sickness or disease in heaven, we expect miracles and healing to occur when God's kingdom is revealed. In the same way we need to raise our awareness and expectation level that angels appear when His Kingdom manifests making our present conditions become like heaven's conditions.

There is a time when we know that angels are always present with us, and that is when we worship God. Psalm 22:23 says, *"But You are holy, enthroned in the praises of Israel."* (NKJV) Whenever we worship God, God comes and establishes His Kingdom and angels are there as well worshipping Him with us. Whether we are alone worshipping Jesus, or in a church service we know by God's Word that angels are with us just like we know God's presence is there. We focus on God's presence, but with an understanding that there are possibly a number of different types of heavenly beings besides angels. We know this from John's description of the throne room of God in Revelation 4 and 5.

Even though we are indirectly inviting angels to come and minister to us by praying for God's Kingdom to come on earth or when we worship God, there is one place in Scripture that gives us clarity about whether or not it is okay to seek angelic encounters. Most theologians say that it is wrong to seek angels or to expect angelic visitations. While that is true in the sense that we should always seek Jesus first, if we understand how His Kingdom operates then we understand through His Word that God chooses, out of His sovereignty, to operate frequently through angels. God does not have to use angels or even mankind, but we know from the Bible that He chooses to use angels and people in establishing His dominion on the earth. This happened when Daniel prayed for 21 days and then an angel came with an answer to his prayers as both angels and man co-labored with God (Dan. 10:13).

The passage that shows that we can ask God for angelic reinforcements or for angels to communicate to us, minister to us, protect us and guide us is the story of Manoah (Judges 13). The angel of the Lord appeared to his wife and prophesied to her about her having a son and to name him Samson. When she told her husband about the experience, he was frustrated because he wanted to encounter the angel as well. So this is what Manoah did:

Judges 13:8-9

⁸Then Manoah prayed to the LORD, and said, "O my Lord, please let the Man of God whom You sent come to us again and teach us what we shall do for the child who will be born." ⁹And God listened to the voice of Manoah, and the Angel of God came to the woman again as she was sitting in the field. (NKJV)

Isn't that amazing? God answered the prayer of Manoah and sent an angel to them. Manoah had a pure heart in his request because he wanted to know how to raise his future son Samson. This gives us a Biblical example showing that it is not wrong to ask the Lord for help from angels. We seek Jesus first and ask Him to come, but also we have an awareness and understanding that He might send an angel to perform His will.

One of the most exciting encounters one of our team members has had with angels came on another trip to Brazil. Vineyard pastors Mike and Cherrie Kaylor, who were tired of the status quo of church and desperate for a touch from God, came on a Global Awakening trip to experience exactly what they had been hearing about in our reports and from the testimonies. Their lives have forever been changed. They now have been helping Global Awakening by going to Brazil a few weeks before the rest of the team to help train and equip pastors and churches for the explosion of the Holy Spirit that usually follows when the Global Awakening team comes in. Below is Mike's story of when the anointing of God came upon his life in a powerful way.

"The stories I had heard [from Global Awakening] told of tremendous outpourings of power and impartation. I heard of miracles, signs and wonders that were occurring on Randy's ministry trips. If my hunger was to be addressed, then I needed to go where heaven seemed to be opened. So, I made the arrangements and found myself on my first ministry trip with Randy, headed to Brazil.

"One of the wonderful blessings of being on the trip was the fact that there was a special time set aside for prayer of impartation for the team. As I stood waiting for "my time" to be prayed for, my mind raced with excitement and wonder as I saw people respond to the prayer with a myriad of reactions. I thought to myself, "What if I am the only one in the room that nothing happens to!" Before I could finish the thought, Randy was standing in front of me and was beginning to pray for me as he laid his hand on my forehead. I suddenly found myself on my knees with uncontrollable shaking and my arms flailing all over the place. "What is going on?" I thought to myself. Then I realized I was in a place where I could either go with it or try to stop it. Who in their right mind would try and stop the very answer to years of prayer for more of the reality of God? So I said, "Lord, let it come."

"What happened next was not what I expected; although, to be honest, I had no idea what to expect. A heat started on the inside of me until it consumed my whole body from head to toe. I felt like I was on fire! As this impartation continued I heard the Lord say, "You've wanted it, you've got it!" I felt a strange tingling sensation going into my forehead. My impression was as if an angel was placing his finger in my forehead, which happened three times.

"I began to receive an understanding about the realm of the angelic and of the angels that had been assigned to me. I became acutely aware that there were two extremely tall angels standing directly behind me on my left and on my right. What I saw next was a sight that at first seemed to conflict with my sense of reason. "What was this huge whirlwind type darkness filled with energy and surrounded by angels?" I thought. As I was wondering about what I was seeing I remembered the scripture that my friend Gary Oates had shared about a type of darkness that surrounded the throne. Would I give myself permission to accept the reality that was unfolding right before me? At that point all I could do was bow down on my knees.

Psalm 97:2

²"Clouds and thick darkness surround Him; Righteousness and justice are the foundation of His throne."

"As I opened my eyes, I noticed that the floor around me was being turned into a body of water. Literally! The fire that was upon me so encompassed me that I felt like I had been placed in a pool of water due to the perspiration. And if that was not enough, the impartation continued into the next night as others on the ministry team had to carry me out of the meeting because I was unable to stand, much less walk.

"The next night we were at a large Four Square regional meeting in a small town close to the ocean. The building was made from ceiling to floor out of concrete including the stage. Randy Clark was teaching and the ministry team was sitting on the stage with him. There must have been 2500 people in the building and the people were hungry for God. Randy was making a statement and walked over toward the team and waved his hand in an expression. As I was sitting in front of him a mist came over me from head to foot. I felt a tangible presence cover me. It was like the spray from a waterfall. It was at that point I began to rock back and forth in the chair unable to sit up all the way as if to stay in a bowing position. I felt a surge of energy begin to ignite from deep within me. As Jesus said, "Out of your innermost being will flow rivers of living water." (John 7:38)

"As I rocked, my feet started to take off like I was running. Here I am sitting in a chair on the stage in front of 2500 people and all I can do is rock back and forth and run. Suddenly I had a vision of a large chambered room. An angel had taken me to the entrance and as I looked in I saw that it was filled with angels scurrying around and distracted. As we stepped into the room, all of the angels flew into single file as if to receive a military procession. There was a very large number in place and I heard the angel that was with me say, "These are now yours to command." I was a little startled at that statement. It took me a while to process what I had heard but I soon began to realize that if I were to accomplish all that was in my heart to do, I was going to need a lot of help." (M. Kaylor 2008)

After this experience, Mike was launched into a powerful healing ministry with the ability to see and discern angels. He and his wife

Cherrie have not looked back and continue to see the power of God move mightily in their ministry with signs, wonders and miracles. There has been such abundant fruit that has come from their lives since these experiences. Our hope is that testimonies like these will encourage your faith and heighten your expectation for the same type of encounters with Jesus Christ, His kingdom and with His heavenly host. This chapter helped us lay a foundation by showing what the Bible says about angels, where they are talked about in Scripture, why we should be aware of their presence, and how they operate and function.

CHAPTER 3

ANGELS DEFINED

Ever wonder what the real difference is between cherubim and seraphim? Why do we talk about hosts? Why is an archangel called by a separate name than everyone else? These questions and more will be answered in the following pages. This chapter is merely a glossary of angels. It is in no way meant to be an exhaustive guide to angels and all that they entail. It is, however, intended to be a point of reference and understanding. Although each category or classification of angel is outlined with scriptural backing, there are other instances where angels have interacted here on earth and there is no scriptural backing. This does not mean that these encounters should be dismissed. We are still mere people, searching out the hidden things to bring them to revelation (Deut. 29:29). With that in mind, please read this chapter with an understanding that this is a reference tool, and a guide as you engage in a very natural part of Christian living.

Various Angelic Descriptions

Before we look at different classes of angels lets look at the terms given regarding angels in the Greek and Hebrew. This list will give understanding to some of the roles that each of the types of angels fulfill. *Leitourgos* (Greek) and *mishrathim* (Hebrew), sometimes used to mean "angels," are the words for "servant" or "minister".

*Host is the Hebrew word *sava*. This encompasses the whole array of God's heavenly army – a military force to fight His battles and accomplish His will. We know from previous chapters that the number of hosts that are in existence is a number larger than most of us have fathomed.

*Watchers, as in Daniel 4:13 and 17, define angels as supervisors and agents employed by God in the affairs of the world. Perhaps this rank of angel is involved in decision making and carrying out God's decrees in earthly matters.

Bene elim, or "sons of the almighty," is translated "O ye mighty" in Psalm 29:1. It is descriptive of the great power of angels.

Bene elohim, or "sons of God," defines angels as a certain class of being. This term includes Satan.

Elohim by itself is only rarely applied to angels. It pictures angels as a supernatural class of beings higher in strength than natural man. When the angels appeared to Jacob at Bethel, the term used is *elohim* (Gen. 35:7).

*Stars is a symbolic term for angels, implying their residence in the heavens (Rev. 12:4). (T. Law 1994:114)

Although this is considered symbolic I have seen several "shooting" stars while driving, or while on walks at night, and have had angelic encounters almost immediately after each of these sightings. One night while driving to Colorado, where I was going to be ministering at a church the next morning, I saw a large star shoot straight in front of me in the sky. I had been asking God to show me a sign about what I felt He was going to release, specifically in the form of angelic support. The next day I saw many angels show up to release healing in the church where I was ministering. I knew that the star the night before was a link, almost as if the angels were going before me to prepare the way.

Rank and Sphere of Influence...

Although angels do not have a serial number, there does appear to be rank and classification. This not only is true of those operating in the heavenly realm of what is considered the "third" heaven, but also of those operating in the "second" heaven, or under the domain of Satan.

As mentioned previously, there are major spheres of influence or classes that an angel can operate in. We know from our foundational definition, not all angels will look like we expect or function the way tradition has taught us. Angels are defined as messengers, but they are also defined as spirit beings. For this chapter when we are talking about angels we will be referencing those that are messengers or have specific assignments on earth, given by God. There will be other "angelic beings" we will discuss, but those are more defined by their spirit "body." What follows are the rank or category angels can fall into, and how they operate within those ranks.

Concerning rank Billy Graham says "they are organized in terms of authority and glory" (T.Law 1994:113). Many others believe that it is based on responsibility given from God. There does however appear to be a constant, while some have more power and authority, all are in the same position of serving and worshiping God, and partnering with us.

Major Categories:

Hosts:

Hosts seems to be the most common term for angels, although there are many facets even within this category. Terry Law writes this about Hosts:

> "The "heavenly hosts" or the multitudes of angels who live in the heavens are also spoken of in military terms. As such, they are an extension of the power and providence of Jehovah of hosts. God is pictured as the "sovereign commander of a great heavenly army who works all His pleasure in heaven and in earth" (1 Sam. 17:45; Ps. 89:6, 8). It also seems then that angels live in the heavenlies and "work" there and on the earth." (T. Law 1994:112)

These angels carry out a number of tasks that will be described later. They also appear to work in conjunction with archangels.

Archangels:

Archangels are the highest ranking angel in the spirit realm. They are the messengers and defenders of God. In her book Third Heaven, Angels, and Other Stuff..., Patricia King says this: "Chief princes or archangels are given jurisdiction over land and special events. Michael is referred to in the Scriptures as an archangel or chief prince. (see Jude 1:9 and Dan 10:13). It is believed that Michael oversees warfare and is the chief prince over the affairs of Israel". The actual word archangel suggests that they are a covering angel (arc), meaning that they give covering or oversight to the rest of the angels. This could be applied to their primary task as messengers. They are the ones that oversee or cover over, the messages of God sent to earth and man. Ezekiel 28 would support this interpretation of the archangel being one that covers. It states about Lucifer, "you were the anointed cherub who covers". There is a responsibility placed on archangels to cover over, and to watch for what God has put in their care.

Although there are three angels in scripture that appear to have the rank of archangel, Michael is the only one who is specifically called that. Gabriel appears to be the main messenger from God. In Luke 1:19 Gabriel says: "I am Gabriel, who stands in the presence of God, and I was sent to speak to you and to bring you this good news" (ESV). Lucifer also appears to be an archangel, however this was before his fall. The high rank that Lucifer held before his fall gives some insight into how the demonic realm is set up. God as the creator is the only one that has the ability to establish hierarchy since before creation. The status of Archangel also allows us to understand the supreme authority of God over all. He is not an archangel, but rather the one true God. The one that is being worshiped and sending these angels. Although, Lucifer is trying to gain an equal footing with God, that can never be because he is a creature and not Creator. There are many other beliefs about Lucifer and his role as an archangel, and many other insights that can be gleaned from this area of study in the Bible.

Although there is a belief in some of the orthodox faiths (Coptic, Eastern and Russian) that there are many named angels, there are only 3 mentioned by name in the Bible. These are the only three that appear to hold this designation of archangel. There are some ministers who believe that this rank of angel is true in the second heaven only, and that in the third heaven there is a different ranking system. Although there is no literal scriptural evidence to back this opinion, it is an interesting concept to consider.

Seraphim:
Isaiah 6 gives great insight into the role of Seraphim.

1 In the year of King Uzziah's death I saw the Lord sitting on a throne, lofty and exalted, with the train of His robe filling the temple. 2 Seraphim stood above Him, each having six wings: with two he covered his face, and with two he covered his feet, and with two he flew. 3 And one called out to another and said, "Holy, Holy, Holy, is the LORD of hosts, The whole earth is full of His glory." 4 And the foundations of the thresholds trembled at the voice of him who called out, while the temple was filling with smoke.

5 Then I said, "Woe is me, for I am ruined! Because I am a man of unclean lips, And I live among a people of unclean lips; For my eyes have seen the King, the LORD of hosts." 6 Then one of the seraphim flew to me with a burning coal in his hand, which he had taken from the altar with tongs. 7 He touched my mouth {with it} and said, "Behold, this has touched your lips; and your iniquity is taken away and your sin is forgiven. "Then I heard the voice of the Lord, saying, "Whom shall I send, and who will go for Us?" Then I said, "Here am I. Send me!" (Isaiah 6:1-7)

The title Seraphim is the plural of the word "seraph". This word means "burning one". As Isaiah describes their role in the throne room, it is interesting that as they cry out "holy, holy, holy", they are also burning ones. James Goll says this about that distinct role of Seraphim:

"The seraphim cry "holy, holy, holy" to each other all the time – and they bring purity to sinful human beings so that we can approach the throne of God. I think that when we experience the manifest presence of God and feel utterly undone and small, the seraphim have been released to come into our realm." (J. W. Goll 2007:59)

As the word "holy" is constantly repeated, there is a declaration of that which is available and that which must prevail because of who and what God is. When the "burning ones" say this, a cleansing is released to eradicate the sins of man that stand opposed to the very nature of God in His holiness. Because of their role in the Third Heaven realm, some ministers would argue that they hold the highest rank. There are different ways to approach this matter. Using Billy Graham's statement about proximity to the Glory we would conclude that the seraphim are the highest. Evaluating it based on authority, the archangels are given special authority to carry out and deliver the message of God on the earth. That is a powerful assignment given to the archangel. The bottom line is that there is no clearly defined understanding of ranking. This is the best interpretation of scriptures that we have at this time. This should inspire you to do your own further research to come to your own conclusion based on the teaching of the Holy Spirit through Scripture.

Cherubim:

Cherubim are referenced 58 times in the Bible. The first reference is in Genesis 3:24, "So He drove the man out; and at the east of the garden of Eden He stationed the cherubim and the flaming sword which turned every direction to guard the way to the tree of life". We know from this first interaction that one of the things that the cherubim do is to stand guard on the orders of God. They are in a sense guardians.

This concept of guardian is further supported later in Ezekiel 10:1-20 where we continue to see the cherubim as the guardians.

Then I looked, and behold, in the expanse that was over the heads of the cherubim something like a sapphire stone, in appearance resembling a throne, appeared above them. And He spoke to the man clothed in linen and said, "Enter between the whirling wheels under the cherubim and fill your hands with coals of fire from between the cherubim and scatter {them} over the city." And he entered in my sight. Now the cherubim were standing on the right side of the temple when the man entered, and the cloud filled the inner court.

Then the glory of the LORD went up from the cherub to the threshold of the temple, and the temple was filled with the cloud and the court was filled with the brightness of the glory of the LORD. Moreover, the sound of the wings of the cherubim was heard as far as the outer court, like the voice of God Almighty when He speaks.

It came about when He commanded the man clothed in linen, saying, "Take fire from between the whirling wheels, from between the cherubim," he entered and stood beside a wheel. Then the cherub stretched out his hand from between the cherubim to the fire which was between the cherubim, took {some} and put {it} into the hands of the one clothed in linen, who took {it} and went out. The cherubim appeared to have the form of a man's hand under their wings.

Then I looked, and behold, four wheels beside the cherubim, one wheel beside each cherub; and the appearance of the wheels {was} like the gleam of a Tarshish stone. As for their appearance, all four of them had the same likeness, as if one wheel were within another wheel. When they moved, they went in {any of} their four directions without turning as they went; but they followed in the direction which they faced, without turning as they went. Their whole body, their backs, their hands, their wings and the wheels were full of eyes all around, the wheels belonging to all four of them. The wheels were called in my hearing, the whirling wheels. And each one had four faces. The first face {was} the face of a cherub, the second face {was} the face of a man, the third the face of a lion, and the fourth the face of an eagle. Then the cherubim rose up. They are the living beings that I saw by the river Chebar. Now when the cherubim moved, the wheels would go beside them; also when the cherubim lifted up their wings to rise from the ground, the wheels would not turn from beside them. When the cherubim stood still, the wheels would stand still; and when they rose up, the wheels would rise with them, for the spirit of the living beings {was} in them.

Then the glory of the LORD departed from the threshold of the temple and stood over the cherubim. When the cherubim departed, they lifted their wings and rose up from the earth in my sight with the wheels beside them; and they stood still at the entrance of the east gate of the LORD'S house, and the glory of the God of Israel hovered over them. These are the living beings that I saw beneath the God of Israel by the river Chebar; so I knew that they {were} cherubim.(NASB)

This passage also gives insight into the role that cherubim play in heaven. Not only are they guardians with specific assignments, but they also have an ability to release God's glory. In Ex.37:9 God directs Moses to place the likeness of these angelic beings on the lid of the ark of the covenant. Once again they are in a "guarding" position. This is not to be confused with "guardian angels", which is a different function that another type of angel plays.

Much like the seraphim, cherubim have wings. Cherubim appear to have 4 wings (Eze 1:6), while seraphim have 6 wings (Is. 6:2). These wings seem to be used for many purposes. Some of the wings appear to be for hiding or shielding the glory of God, or even the coal that carries some of the Glory. They also seem to be an instrument of noise or declaration: *Moreover, the sound of the wings of the cherubim was heard as far as the outer court, like the voice of God Almighty when He speaks.(v.5).* (NASB)

Some theologians differ in opinion of ranking. Although it appears that archangels are the highest in rank because they are *messengers* (the very definition of angel, see chapter 2), others believe that cherubim are the highest because of their responsibility and relation to the glory in the throne room. Regarding the ranking of cherubim, Terry Law says this: Cherubim appear to be the highest rank of the heavenly beings. One reason cherubim are never called angels may be because they are never messengers. They are never used in Scripture to carry revelation of instruction from God to men. They are used to protect God's glory and proclaim his grace" (T. Law 1994:116). With this in mind, it appears that *archangels are the highest of angels, while cherubim are the highest of heavenly beings.*

Living Creatures:
There will not be a lot of time devoted to these particular heavenly beings, except for a few basics to help us gain insight. The living creatures are not angels. They are however heavenly beings in the same sense that angels are "spirit" beings with no distinct body, thus making it hard to describe them in terms of what is natural for human understanding. This is true of all the heavenly beings. Ezekiel 1 gives a clearer description of the living creatures. From this portion of scripture we can glean that the living creatures have four wings, and that they are also connected to the glory of God. The function of the living creatures is one that still is a mystery to most. Law has this to say regarding their function:

"The purpose of the living creatures – whatever they are – seems to be to worship God directly, to witness the worship of God by redeemed men and, in Revelation, to direct the judgments of God" (T. Law 1994:117).

There does appear to be a co-existing of the living creatures and the cherubim. It is almost as if they are one in the same. In Ezekiel 10, the prophet specifically uses the names interchangeably as he describes what is happening around the glory of God.

Wheels:

The wheels, or "the whirling wheels" (Ezek. 10:13), appear to be used to carry the throne of God. Reading the first ten chapters of Ezekiel will give valuable insight into what the function of the wheels are, and even the mechanics of how they work. They appear to move in mysterious ways quite different from our mechanical way of thinking. While the lead wheel moves forward, the rest follow without changing direction. This again brings us to Is. 1:18 "come let us reason together," relying heavily upon the Holy Spirit to be our teacher.

OTHER ANGELS:

Although, we have looked at the specific roles that angels fulfill (and other heavenly beings, those that are not "messengers"), it is important to review some of the common ways that angels have been used on the earth toward man. When there is not a good understanding of how angels have interacted with people in the past, there is a potential to miss how they might act in the future. It would be a tragedy to miss appointed times and seasons in your life where God wants to meet you!

Angels of Light (Angels of Deception):

"An 'angel of light' in biblical terms is not an angel that appears in a burst of light or looks radiant or has a halo around his head. An angel of light, regardless of what he looks like, says or does, is a spirit who presents a gospel other than what is found in the Bible" (T. Law 1994:47)

An angel of light, therefore, is one that allures you with a false gospel.

"But though we, or an angel from heaven, preach any other gospel unto you than that which we have preached unto you, let him be accursed (Gal. 1:8 NASB).

As previously mentioned (chapter 2), this angel is a messenger from Satan trying to deliver a message of false doctrine. Not only is that the intent, but it has been successful in its mission many times. Both Islam and Mormonism have been a bi-product of such a "angelic visitation" (T. Law 1994:49).

Influences of the Angel of Light can be seen in other religious sects that have become very popular in recent years. This would include Kabbalah (a mixture of neo-spiritualism and Jewish beliefs). This movement is earmarked by the leading of angels and demonic beings, and have developed an intricate hierarchy of angels by their followers. Kabbalah has heavily influenced many in the Hollywood culture in recent years. The increase of interest in angels is predictable. The yearning for guidance and feelings of spiritual enlightenment has increased in value in western society. As a result many are turning to New Age, Psychics, Aura Readers and "Seers" to receive guidance and have their questions answered. In these times of growing tensions on the earth (in the Middle East especially), it is important to understand that the Angel of Light has had a long reaching impact. The modern church cannot ignore this. Now, more than ever, it is vital to know, understand and live the true gospel of Jesus Christ (T. Law 1994: ch 5).

Guardian Angels (angels on assignment):

The question of guardian angels has long been one that is disputed. While the new age world has, in a sense, "cornered the market" on this area of angelic classification, the church has done very little to address it. In earlier chapters there was reference to this particular function of angels. Both Matt. 18:10, and Acts 12 were referenced as biblical foundation for these guardian angels. Also, previously it has been established that the cherubim have a role in guarding the Glory of God. Colossians 1:27 establishes "Christ, in you, the hope of glory", meaning that Christ in us is the hope of glory on this earth. We are the hope of the glory of God being realized again. If God has established a guardianship in the heavens for his glory, would he not establish a guardianship of his glory on the earth also?

In Acts 12, Peter gets released from prison. When he goes to the house where the other disciples are meeting there is a misunderstanding. Rhoda tells the disciples that Peter is at the door, they respond "you must have seen his angel". While this particular passage raises many questions, it does however confirm that there are angels that could pose as personal or "guardian" angels. Later in Revelation 22:16 Jesus says, "I, Jesus, have sent my angel to testify to you these things, for the churches". If Jesus has an angel that he sends, it would make sense for us to also have an angel that we work with.

Both Kenneth Hagin and Oral Roberts have had encounters with angels who delivered personal messages, or performed actions that either kept them in safety or met specific needs. Hagin had an encounter where both Jesus and an angel appeared to him. The following is an account of the interaction that occurred in 1963:

"Hagin's first question to Jesus was, 'Who is that fellow?'
He says that Jesus answered very specifically, 'He's your angel.'

Hagin asked, 'What do you mean, he's my angel?'

He said Jesus quoted Matthew 18:10, the foundational verse for most belief in guardian angels.

In that verse, Jesus told the disciples that the angels of 'these little ones' always behold the face of God.

Hagin said that Jesus added, 'You don't lose your angel just because you grow up'" (T. Law 1994:72-73).

Hagin goes on to describe the rest of the encounter, how the angel gave encouragement and counsel for current situations that were happening in his life. He states that the angel gave specific direction for his life, including details which helped him avoid a possible downfall in an upcoming financial deal.

Another young girl whose sister attended our ministry school, the Global School of Supernatural Ministry (GSSM), had a most incredible experience with what appeared to be guardian angels, who no longer had an assignment. Deborah was only 14. This is the account that she wrote, several months after the encounter happened:

"It was the summer of 2006, I was 14 years old, and my church had planned a youth meeting at a local park in Westminster, MD. Two or three other churches had been invited to this meeting, but not all of them believed in tongues or the gifts of the spirit. Before the meeting started my friends and I went over to a place where people couldn't see us to pray for the meeting. While we were praying I started speaking in tongues and could not stop. I also started doing hand gestures as if I were telling little kids what to do. My pastor wanted to be sensitive to the people who didn't understand what was going on, so he asked me to try to keep it down a little bit – or at least stop the hand movements, but I couldn't. Ten or fifteen minutes went by, and it was now time to go eat hamburgers and hot dogs before the meeting started. While everybody was eating, I couldn't just sit down anymore. I was still speaking in tongues. I felt like I should go over to the other side of the pavilion we were in. As I walked over to the other side, I noticed that there were angels lined up throughout the place we were in. I started going from angel to angel, naming them and telling them where they were going and what their mission was. After doing this I looked outside of the pavilion and saw thousands and thousands of angels. Worship was about to start, so I headed back to the other side where everybody else was and tried to worship a little bit. This time worship was different. For some reason I couldn't focus. I felt like I should go back outside, so I did. I sat at a picnic table right outside of our pavilion. A little angel came and sat next to me. We talked for a little bit. I told him my life story - still in tongues - and he told me his. He said those angels I was seeing, including him, were the angels of aborted babies. Because the babies were killed so early on in their lives their angels never got to complete their mission on the earth. But now they were coming back to help us intercede and fight for the lives of the little ones who are still to come, and end abortion all throughout the world. As soon as he told me that, I could speak English again. I went back in and told my pastor what had just happened, and the meeting went on. I've seen these angels a number of times ever since I saw them that day at the park, and I know there are many more to come."

OTHER ROLES ANGELS CAN FULFILL:

There are other roles that angels fulfill. These are not necessarily defining roles for them. Just as we have looked at different forms of angelic encounter, this is a summary of roles that we can expect them to fulfill.

- Angels are protectors of believers (Ps. 34:7)

- Angels are partners in spiritual warfare (Rev. 12:7-11)
- Angels are assigned as "heavenly evangelists" (Rev.14:15, Matt. 13:38 & 39)
- Angels bring divine strength (Matt. 4:11)
- Angels deliver messages (Matt. 1:20)
- Angels can be the catalyst for healing (John 5:1-4)
- Angels release financial blessing and prosperity (Ps. 103:20 – do the "bidding" of God) (T. Bentley 2005: 158-164)

Even though angels have specific roles that they fulfill, and spheres of influence that they are in charge of, they also can have varied jobs within those parameters. Hopefully this will give you a baseline of expectation and understanding for angelic activity in your own life!

Angels are a mysterious part of the Christian life. There are still many unanswered questions. The best way to learn more is to have your own encounters and to enter into this world with an open heart. Oh, and One last story….

The first year of our school (GSSM), the students were learning a lot about character and how that relates to ministry. One young man was taking a year off from being a youth pastor with his wife to come to the school. To my knowledge he had never had an angelic encounter before, and was not on any kind of special fast at this particular moment in time. It was about half way through the school year and he had fallen asleep on the couch one winter evening. He woke up in the middle of the night. He was immediately aware of his surroundings, where he was and what was going on around him. He noticed a glow in the corner of the room and he quickly turned his attention in that direction. As he connected with the glow, he saw an angel standing before him. The angel had come to deliver a message to him. The angel went on to discuss with this young man the importance of character and holiness. According to the student this went on for most of the night. At the time he could not give specifics of what the angel had said, but conveyed the seriousness of the message to the rest of the students. Then the class responded to the word and moved into a time of prayer for this message to become manifest in their lives. I am not aware if the young man has had any other angelic visitations, but I know that he will never be the same after that encounter, and neither will our other students.

After so many stories, insights, biblical foundations, it's time to put to practice what has been taught. You are commissioned to enter into the world of encounter, go for it, don't hold back, and be amazed at what God has in store for you. Right after our chapter on Q & A, we'll talk about preparing ourselves to interact with the unseen spiritual realm.

CHAPTER 4

ANGELS Q & A

I have included this chapter because, like you, I have had and still have my share of questions about the angelic and partnering with them. I remember hearing Randy's account of talking with his Brazilian friend, Davi Silva, and asking the burning question: "Are we supposed to command angels?" Davi replied that he didn't know, but he'd ask. To Randy's surprise, he turned his head for a few moments, looked back at him and said, "Randy, they say you don't have to command a friend."

I have decided to include this chapter because not all of us can turn to our right or left and ask our guardian angel all the questions we have. In it, I describe what the Word of God says about some of the most common, significant and controversial questions about angels.

In the Kingdom, are angels of higher or lower rank than man?

Psalm 8:4-5 says,

What is man that You are mindful of him, And the son of man that You visit him? For You have made him a little lower than the angels, and You have crowned him with glory and honor. (KJV)

From this, it seems as if this passage is in conflict with Paul, who writes in I Corinthians 6:3, speaking of the millennial reign, "Do you not know that we shall judge angels…?" How can one judge when they're in a lower position?

The NASB version has another interpretation of the passage in Psalm 8. It reads, "What is man that You take thought of Him? And the son of man that You care for him? Yet You made him a little lower than God, and You crowned him with glory and majesty!" In his book, Working with Angels, Steven Brooks attributes this misinterpretation to the early writers being too shocked to translate it correctly.

It seems to me that when the early translators of the King James Version encountered verse 5 of Psalm chapter 8, they were quite possibly stunned by the literal Hebrew translation. The literal translation of this verse may have been too far beyond their ability to comprehend; therefore, they employed human intervention and changed the wording to something that they deemed to be more "realistic" (Brooks 2007:28).

If you look at the original Hebrew language, the verse says exactly: "Yet You made him a little lower than Elohim." Brooks continues,

"It may be hard for some to grasp this truth, and certainly the King James translators did the best they could with the understanding they had in their day and time…but the more one studies the Word of God, the truth becomes quite evident that man was created just a shade lower than God Himself" (Brooks 2007:29).

In fact, according to Strong's Exhaustive Concordance, the Hebrew word is used 2,606 times in the KJV. Exactly 2,591 of those are translated as God. This is the only time in scripture we read Elohim translated as angels.

If you continue reading in Psalm 8, verse 6 explains much more.

Yet You made him a little lower than God, And You crowned him with glory and majesty! You make him to rule over the words of Your hands; **You have put all things under his feet…** *(Psalm 8:5-6 NASB, emphasis mine).*

When God created man, he made us in His image (Gen 1:27) to rule and have dominion. Psalm 115:16 says that "The heavens are the heavens of the Lord, but the earth He has given to the sons of men." We don't have time in this short section to unpack this more, but Scripture is clear that God has honored us, which means He's lifted us up to His level. Are we like God? Of course not! But didn't Jesus quote the Psalms saying "Has it not been written in your Law, 'I said, you are gods'?" (John 10:34 NASB).

How many archangels are there?

I have heard different numbers from different sources. According to the canonized version of the Bible, Michael is the only angel ever named an archangel. (Note: for more on this, reference Chapter 3, Classification of Angels). His name literally means, "who is like unto the Lord." There is also biblical proof that Lucifer was once an archangel before his fall, possibly the highest. And although it is never mentioned as such, I believe Gabriel is an archangel as well. His name literally means, "God is great," and he is best known as a messenger of the Lord. In Luke 1:19, Gabriel introduces himself as one "who stands in the presence of God." Again, this is all we can extract from the canon of Scripture.

Other books, however, note different names in addition to Michael and Gabriel. I have not written this book to try to attest to the validity of the non-canonized books, so please understand that these other archangel names are not Scriptural, merely tradition and what we can see from these other books. Many Jewish, Eastern Orthodox, and Catholic scholars identify the seven spirits before the throne of God in Revelation 1:4 as seven archangels.

In addition to Michael and Gabriel, we read about Raphael, whose names mean, "God has healed." There are a few references to him in the Book of Tobit, a deutero-canonical book of the Apocrypha. Jewish tradition widely believes that it is the archangel Raphael who is the "angel of the Lord" who stirred the waters at certain seasons at the pool of Bethesda in John 5.

Uriel will appear in II Esdras, a non-canonical book, instructing the prophet Ezra after he inquired of God. In the Book of Enoch, another non-canonical book, Uriel is responsible for communicating to Noah about the great flood. Uriel's name means, "Fire of God."

"Friend of God" is the meaning of the fifth archangel, Raguel. Tradition refers to Raguel as being the archangel of justice, fairness, and harmony. You can find references to Raguel in the Book of Enoch, specifically as the angel who escorted Enoch to and from heaven during his visits.

Zerachiel, or "God's Command," is one of the angels who carries out God's judgment on the earth.

Lastly, we have Ramiel. His name means "Thunder of God." You can find references to him in the Book of Enoch.

Jewish, Orthodox, Catholic, and other traditions name Salathiel ("Prayer to God"), Jehudiel ("Praise of God"), and Barachiel ("Blessing of God") and many other named archangels.

I would like to make it clear again that these names are not from Scripture, rather from tradition or extra-canonical books in history. I don't know if we'll ever know names or numbers of the archangels in this time, or if we really need to. I like best what the Apostle Paul wrote to the Ephesians' church in Eph 1:19-21 (emphasis mine),

> *These are in accordance of the working of the strength of His might which He brought about in Christ, when He raised Him from the dead and seated Him at his right hand in the heavenly places, far above all rule and authority and power and dominion, and **every name that is named, not only in this age but also in the one to come**. (NASB)*

Who, or what, is the "Angel of the Lord?"
Rabbi Loren Jacobs, former staff member for Jews for Jesus, writes:

"Since the time of Abraham, our people have known about the angels of the Lord. In the Talmud he is given the name Metatarsus, which indicates a special relationship with God. One meaning of meta and thronos, two Greek words, gives the sense of "one who serves behind the throne of God." He is also known as the "Prince of the Countenance" because of the close proximity between this angel and God Himself. The implication for the malakh of the Lord is that He is, above all, the messenger of God, the one sent by God, the one who represents God Himself" (Jacobs 1983).

The angel of the Lord has been a great mystery to many people. In an attempt not to start preaching a fourth person of the trinity, let's look at some references in Scripture where we see the angel of the Lord.

Genesis 16, after Hagar had fled from Sarai to the desert, is the first time we meet the angel. It was the angel of the Lord who found her in vs. 7 by the spring on the way to Shur and asked where she was going. The angel of the Lord continued on to tell her about her son's name and about his descendants. Here's how Hagar reacted after receiving the prophetic word:

Then she called the name of the Lord who spoke to her, "You are a God who sees"; for she said, "Have I even remained alive here after seeing Him?" (Gen 16:13 NASB).

Hagar equated seeing the angel as seeing God. In fact, she even heard him as if she were hearing God, as in vs. 10 where the angel said to her, "I will greatly multiply your descendants…" The angel of the Lord who delivered this message to Sarai's servant is the same one who appears to give Sarai's husband an almost identical message.

Before we get to Abraham, I want to point something out something else that occurred. Hagar wasn't the only person to make such a "mistake." In Judges 6, Gideon had an encounter with the angel of the Lord who told him he was the chosen one to deliver Israel from Midian. We don't need to go into the whole story, but Gideon's reaction after the angel of the Lord vanished is interesting.

When Gideon saw that he was the angel of the Lord, he said, "Alas, O Lord God! For now I have seen the angel of the lord face to face." The Lord said to him, "Peace be to you, do not fear; you shall not die." Then Gideon built an altar there to the Lord… (Judges 6:22-24a NASB).

Like Hagar, Gideon equated seeing the angel of the Lord with seeing the Lord Himself. Jacob had the same response when he wrestled with the "man" who changed his name in Genesis 32. In vs. 30 Jacob is surprised and says, "I have seen God face to face, yet my life has been preserved." Now, here this passage doesn't explicitly say the "man" was the angel of the Lord, but I think it's safe to assume that Jacob must have understood something about him that scripture doesn't say. Why else would he react the way he did?

Jacob, Gideon, and Hagar all had the same reaction to seeing the angel of the Lord: "I have seen God face to face." It must have been known that seeing the Lord face to face would result in death, either through Moses' law that Gideon knew, or an understanding during Abraham, Isaac, and Jacob's time.

Now, let's take a look at Abraham's encounter with the angel of the Lord. When Abraham went up the mount to sacrifice Isaac in Genesis 22, it was the angel of the Lord who called out for him to stop. It's interesting to note that in vs. 11 and again in vs. 15 it clearly says that the angel of the Lord called out to Abraham from heaven. Why wouldn't the author just say that God spoke from heaven? Instead, there's a distinction made between the angel of the Lord and the Lord Himself, as when God told Abraham to sacrifice his son in vss. 1 and 2. In this passage, there are four different "characters" who speak, if you will. First, there's God. Secondly, Abraham. Third to speak is Isaac, asking about the missing sacrifice. And lastly, it's the angel of the Lord. It was the angel who gave Abraham the message to spare his son.

> *But the angel of the Lord called to him from heaven and said, "Abraham, Abraham!" And he said, "Here I am." He said, "Do not stretch out your hand against the lad, and do nothing to him; for now I know that you fear God, since you have not withheld your son, your only son, from Me" (Gen 22:11,12 NASB).*

And again…

> *Then the angel of the Lord called to Abraham a second time from heaven, and said, "By Myself I have sworn, declares the Lord, because you have done this and not withheld your son, your only son, indeed I will greatly bless you, and I will greatly multiply your seed as the stars of the heavens and as the sand which is on the seashore; and your seed shall possess the gate of their enemies. In your seed all the nations of the earth shall be blessed, because you have obeyed My voice" (Gen 22:15-18 NASB).*

Notice how the angel speaks. He told Abraham he knew Abraham feared God, not because he didn't withhold his son from God, but "from Me" (vs 12).

Throughout the Old Testament, there are over 60 references specifically to the angel of the Lord. We will not look at every one of them, but you can see some of them for yourself. You can find more in Gen 21:17-18, Exod 3:2, Num 22:22-38, Judges 2:1-4, 5:23, 13:3-22, 2 Samuel 24:16, Zech 1:12, 3:1 and 12:8. However, you will not find a single reference or appearance to <u>the</u> angel of the Lord in the New Testament.

A reason we don't read about the angel of the Lord in the New Testament is that the angel of the Lord is a theophany, or a physical manifestation of God the Father. In Gen. 18, Abraham greets three visitors in an unusual way...

Now the Lord appeared to him [Abraham] by the oaks of Mamre, while he was sitting at the tent door in the heat of the day. When he lifted up his eyes and looked, behold, three men were standing opposite him; and when he saw them, he ran from the tent door to meet them and bowed himself to the earth, and said, "My Lord, if now I have favor in Your sight, please do not pass Your servant by" (Gen 18:1-3 NASB).

Wouldn't you say that is an odd way to greet travelers passing in front of your home? Not if you recognized God in one of them. Later, as these three men sit and eat with Abraham, and one tells him about his future son. Verse 13 reveals the identity of one of the men...

And the Lord said to Abraham, "Why did Sarah laugh...?" (NASB)

Several times in the following passages, it's repeated that "the Lord said..." While it is never said that the angel of the Lord visited Abraham to speak to him, we can see that God Himself came and visited Abraham.

In Exodus 3, Moses starts off having a conversation with the angel of the Lord. But before long he finds himself talking directly with God Himself. Speaking of Moses, who was it that led him and the Israelites through the wilderness in a cloud of smoke by day and a pillar of fire by night in Exodus 13? In Genesis 3:8, it is written that Adam and Eve "heard the sound of the Lord God walking in the garden in the cool of the day." Was it a physical sound? Whose footsteps were they hearing? Could it be possible that they witnessed a theophany, a physical manifestation of

God? Could it have been He that led the way in the wilderness, or sat with Abraham, or walked with Adam and Eve? I do not have all the answers, but I know that God is certainly big enough to do whatever He wants!

Something else to consider is that the angel is a pre-incarnation of Jesus Christ, or christophany. In John 8:58 Jesus states, "Truly, truly, I say to you, before Abraham was born, I am." But if he didn't show up on the earth until he was announced to Mary, then where was He? What was He doing? Was He just floating around, waiting for His cue? I strongly doubt it. John 1 starts off with a familiar passage:

> *In the beginning was the Word, and the Word was with God, and the Word was God.* **He was in the beginning with God.** *All things came into being through Him, and apart from Him nothing came into being that has come into being (John 1:1-3 NASB, emphasis mine).*

And later…

> *And the Word became flesh, and dwelt among us, and we saw His glory, glory as of the only begotten from the Father, full of grace and truth. John testified about Him and cried out, saying, "This was He of whom I said, He who comes after me has a higher rank than I, for He existed before me" (John 1:14-15 NASB, emphasis mine).*

We must not forget that this man, this Word became flesh, is eternally Jesus. He existed with God the Father before the very beginning of it all. Moreover, of God the Father, this is written: "No one has seen God at any time; the only begotten God who is in the bosom of the Father, He has explained Him" (John 1:18 NASB). Jesus came to explain God the Father to us. Because it was God the Father who told Moses, "You cannot see My face, for no man can see Me and live" (Exod 33:20 NASB). But how can that be? The Old Testament is full of encounter after encounter with the angel of the Lord, who is the Lord Himself. Did Hagar, Abraham, Jacob, Moses, and others somehow find a "loophole" to God's decree? I think not, because David wrote that "You have magnified Your word above all Your name" (Psalm 138:2c NASB). I would propose that the reason we don't read about the angel of the Lord in the New Testament is because the Lord does not appear as an angel anymore, but Jesus Christ in the flesh. Today, Jesus' ministry is still alive and active. We no longer "need" the angel of the Lord; we need Jesus. Hebrews 1:1-2 says,

> God, after He spoke long ago to the fathers in the prophets in many portions and in many ways, **in these last days has spoken to us in His Son**, whom He appointed heir of all things, through whom also He made the world (NASB).

These verses, which are so often misquoted and misused as an argument for why prophecy doesn't exist today, are attesting to the unlimited nature of God. He chose to speak to mankind any way He wanted, in many different varieties of ways. If He wanted to send His Son "before His time," God could have. If He wanted to show up on the earth as a cloud of smoke, He could have done that, too.

Can people be "touched by an angel," especially in the area of healing?
    I believe so. Here's why: if demonic spirits (which I believe are fallen angels) can afflict a person with sickness, why couldn't angels touch a person with God's anointing and bring healing? If a fallen angel can go into a person, then an "un-fallen" angel can do the same. Fallen angels have perverted their gift of health to bring sickness. We read of many times when Jesus rebuked the demons, telling them to "come out" of an afflicted person. They have to be in to come out!

    In the Old Testament, we read about countless people who were filled with different spirits. Deut 34:9 says, "Now Joshua the son of Nun was filled with the spirit of wisdom, for Moses had laid his hands on him…(NASB)" Now, it certainly can be argued that this spirit of wisdom (or of understanding, revelation, faith, etc.) can be the Holy Spirit, but let me ask the same question the writer of Hebrews asked. "Are they [angels] not all ministering spirits, sent out to render service for the sake of those who will inherit salvation?" (Heb 1:14 NASB). Is it possible to think that those spirits could be angels?

    In 2007, I was in Brazil and saw an angel of God literally put his hands inside a woman who had lung cancer. I say had cancer because the woman was healed! As soon as I saw this happen, the woman fell to the floor. When she came to, all of the intense pain that was in her chest had ceased. I hear about countless testimonies about the "storehouses" of heaven, that are filled with new body parts, like legs, arms, hearts, lungs (like this woman), and anything else that makes up the human body. How would these body parts come down to our realm and be placed inside of the person being healed unless an angel does it? I believe God uses them in healing as He uses us in healing. Angels carry anointing just as we do.

In the end, I'll admit that I don't have all the answers. But I think there's more danger in dismissing questions like this because they're different and new than in tackling the issue. In a recent Global Awakening conference, called Voice of the Prophets, Patricia King made the following statement concerning the same question:

> "It's an interesting topic, and I don't think we should be afraid of thinking about it, even if we don't come to any conclusions. It's one of those things that doesn't really matter, does it? But it's kind of intriguing to think about it. I'd encourage you to think about it, and be talking about it, instead of just saying, "NO! That cannot be!" Explore possibilities; think of the great possibilities of God. I'm not quite sure yet how I believe…but I like thinking about the greatness of God and I like thinking about the possibility of having an angel ministering inside, maybe shuffling parts around or something…I don't know! I like the idea of that. I think it's ok that we can think about this with God. He says, come reason together with Him, and say, "God, do you *do* stuff like that? Can you show me?" Instead of being shocked by a thought" (VOP 2008).

And so, I'd encourage the same. Keep exploring, and just keep an open mind and an open heart.

What are the three heavens, and in which do angels exist and operate?

In recent years, there's been a lot of mention of the "third heaven." What is the third heaven, and what does it have to do with the angelic? And what happened to the first two heavens, did we just skip over them? We first hear the phrase "third heaven" when Paul writes that, "I know a man in Christ who fourteen years ago – whether in the body I do not know, or out of the body I do not know, God knows – such a man was caught up to the *third heaven*" (2 Cor 12:2 NASB, emphasis mine). Most scholars agree that Paul is writing concerning his own visionary experience. So what is Paul referring to when he says third heaven?

First, let's take a look at what leads up to the third heaven. Obviously, if Paul mentions a third one, there's a first and second heaven as well. Isaiah writes,

*For thus says the Lord, who created the **heavens** (He is the God who formed the earth and made it, He established it and did not create it as a waste place, but formed it to be inhabited)...(Isaiah 45:18 NASB, emphasis mine).*

And again...

*The **heaven**, even the **heavens**, are the Lord's; But the earth he has given to the children of men (Psalm 115:16, NKJV, emphasis mine).*

In all three uses of the word heaven, the same Hebrew word is used. The word *shamayim*, (pronounced shaw-mah'-yim) can mean: a) the sky; b) the abode of the stars and the visible universe (sky, atmosphere, etc); or c) heaven, the abode of God. So, if Gen 1:1 tell us that in the beginning God created the heavens (plural) and the earth, what levels did he create? We just saw the answer: the sky around us, the stars and physical universe and God's home. In Gen 1:8, we see how God separated one expanse of waters from another, this he called heaven. Thus, we have the first heaven: the created earth and its atmosphere. Even in Gen 1:26, the word *shamayim* is used:

*Then God said, "Let Us make man in Our image, according to Our likeness; and let them rule over the fish of the sea and over the birds **of the sky** and over the cattle and over all the earth, and over every creeping thing that creeps on the earth" (NASB).*

Here, the same word is used, therefore establishing the earth and its atmosphere as the first of the three heavens. It's the realm where we all see, touch, feel, interact with, and exist. It's the realm that the disciples were staring at when Jesus ascended into the clouds out of their sight.

*And as they were gazing intently into the sky while He was going, behold, two men in white clothing stood beside them. They also said, "Men of Galilee, why do you stand looking up into **the sky**? This Jesus, who has been taken up from you **into heaven**, will come in just the same way as you have watched Him go **into heaven**" (Acts 1:10-11 NASB).*

In this case, we have the disciples staring off into the sky (some translations use the word heaven), and these two men show up. The Greek word used in this passage has the same definition as the Hebrew word for heaven. So who were these two men? I think by now it's safe to say that these two men were angels sent by God. So, this verse tells us two things: what the disciples saw and experienced in the natural was in the first of these heavens – the sky – and that angels exist and move among us in this heaven.

Next, we have the heaven of space; the second heaven. The Bible makes many references to this realm even though it never specifically calls it by that name. So we reach this conclusion by inference, but our case is a strong one. Let's go back to Gen 22, where Abraham received the promise about his descendant. He was told that he would be blessed, and his seed multiplied as the stars of the heavens (Gen 22:17). It's important to note the usage of the word *shamayim* here as well. Although in this case it is not likened to the sky or the earth, as we saw before, but to the stars and constellations.

> *Can you bind the chains of the Pleiades, or loose the cords of Orion? Can you lead forth a constellation in its season, and guide the Bear with her satellites? Do you know the ordinances of the* **heavens***, or fix their rule over the earth? (Job 38:31-33 NASB).*

It is of this realm that God commanded the Israelites to "…beware not to lift up your eyes to heaven and see the sun and the moon and the stars, all the host of heaven, and be drawn away and worship them, those which the Lord your God has allotted to all the peoples under the whole heaven" (Deut 4:19). So, while the Lord established this second heaven, there's nothing in it worthy of worship. Obviously, there must be a higher realm.

It is in the second heaven where much spiritual warfare happens. The account in Rev. 12 is an interesting passage.

> *And there was a war in heaven, Michael and his angels waging war with the dragon. The dragon and his angels waged war, and they were not strong enough, and there was no longer a place found for them in heaven (Rev 12:7-8 NASB).*

We see that both angels of God and angels of darkness have access and power there. But the dragon (Satan) was cast out even from there.

The second heaven is the realm above the earth, separating this world from God's.

Which brings us to the third heaven or God's home. In Matt 6, Jesus taught us to pray to "our Father, who is in heaven." For a moment, let's continue reading in Paul's account of being caught up…

I know a man in Christ who fourteen years ago – whether in the body I do not know, or out of the body I do not know, God knows – such a man was caught up to the third heaven. And I know how such a man – whether in the body or apart from the body I do not know, God knows – was caught up into Paradise and heard inexpressible words, which a man is not permitted to speak (2 Cor 12:2-4 NASB).

Here, Paul equates the third heaven with Paradise. It's the same Paradise Jesus spoke of to the criminal hanging on the cross next to him in Luke 23:43. This definition of heaven is the last one we mentioned before: the abode of God. Actually, the Greek word used here *Ouranos* (pronounced oo-ran-os'), has more depth than that. Strong's defines it as "the region above the sidereal [concerning the stars, or the second heaven] heavens, the seat of order of things eternal and consummately perfect where God dwells and other heavenly beings."

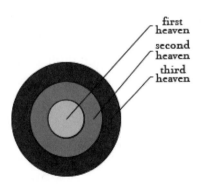

first heaven
second heaven
third heaven

The third heaven is where God is enthroned. There is no darkness in heaven, because "God is Light, and in Him there is no darkness at all" (1 John 1:5 NASB). The enemy, or anything he stands for, cannot exist in the third heaven. It's where the angels worship: "…for I say to you that their **angels in heaven** continually see the face of My Father **who is in**

heaven" (Matt 18:10b NASB, emphasis mine). This is the place of God's dwelling. This third heaven is what John encountered when he entered through the doorway standing open in Revelation 4.

It helps to view these three heavens as three levels. However, this model does not exactly do it justice. They are not exactly three levels in the physical sense. They are really more like three planes of existence, or three realms (each level being able to descend onto the levels below it). So, we cannot be in the third heaven and bring the second with us, but we can be in the third and come live in the first. This is what Jesus meant when He said, "No one has ascended to heaven but He who came down from heaven, that is, the Son of Man who is in heaven" (John 3:13, NKJV). As children of God, we know that we're with Christ, seated in heavenly places (Eph. 1:20, 2:6), and we have access to a realm without demons or darkness, rather full of angelic beings and light. In praying "Your kingdom come, Your will be done, on earth as it is in Heaven," (Matt. 6) we are releasing the third heaven we are from, complete with all the angelic activity and power, into the first and second we are presently in.

How do I deal with and minister to New Agers or Spiritualists who claim to have had encounters with "angels" or spirits?

Interacting with different spirits is normal, sought after, and highly encouraged in new age spiritualism. And we're certainly aware that Satan disguises himself as an angel of light, but this isn't the section for us to discuss discernment. That's already been discussed in previous chapters. Instead, I'd like to focus on another aspect of this argument.

Haggai 2:7 calls the soon-coming Jesus the "Desire of all Nations." Bill Johnson defines this as being the one every heart wants, whether they know it or not. Jesus said, *"...I, if I am lifted up from the earth, will draw all men to Myself"* (John 12:32 NASB). Being created in the image of God, we are wired to search for Him. In all the searching, in all of life, in all of everything, the answer is Jesus. How else would the woman with the issue of blood in Mark 5 have known who Jesus was? She knew him either by reputation or the Scriptures. She could have known from Malachi 4:2 that the Messiah would come with "healing in His wings." (Note: this passage, literally translated, gave everyone the understanding that the Messiah would have healing in the edge of His garments.) If she knew that one, then she might have known Isaiah 53:2 which says, "He has no stately form or majesty that we should look upon Him, nor appearance that we should be attracted to Him." When Jesus came, apparently there wasn't anything desirous about Him, except his ever-growing reputation. Either way, there was something that drew this woman who needed healing to risk her life to meet Him. She was drawn to something in Him. As the "Desire of the Nations," everyone's heart is seeking Him.

That is where, I believe, the New Age has missed it. They are searching for the right thing, they are just finding it in different places. Or, more correctly, not quite finding it. In Scripture we see that all of creation worships Jesus.

> *He [Jesus] is the image of the invisible God, the firstborn of all creation. For by Him all things were created, both in the heavens and on earth, visible and invisible…all things have been created through Him and **for him.** He is before all things, and in Him all things hold together" (Col. 1:15-17 NASB).*

That's why, Bill Johnson explains, the New Age movement has such a value for nature and the environment. It's because they are searching for God in His creation. Is it wrong? Of course. We know that there is only one way to the Father, and that is through Jesus Christ. So I would say that we should follow Jesus' example. Look at the way He dealt with the woman at the well in John 4. Similarly, to the New Agers of today, this woman was misled and following a different path that had both a different end and different means. Instead of condemning her, Jesus did the following three things: 1) validated and empowered her, 2) introduced her to the supernatural, and 3) revealed Himself.

With or without the gift of discernment, it's not hard to guess that probably more often than not a New Ager's encounter will not be with a holy angel. However, it's important to validate and empower your friend. By talking with this woman, Jesus let her know that she was valuable and worth much in His eyes. By recognizing that a New Ager's encounter is real to them, and not dismissing it as gibberish as other Christians may have, you are empowering them to believe in the experience of the supernatural.

Secondly, we need to confront them with our understanding of the supernatural realm. To confront means to come face to face with. It doesn't have to be a negative thing. After validating her, Jesus gave her a word of knowledge about her past. He brought her face to face with a reality that was higher, bigger and different from any she had known. John 8:32 (NASB) says, "and you will know the truth, and the truth will make you free." The word "know" is not speaking of intellectual knowledge, it's about an experiential knowledge. What Jesus is saying is, "You will experience the truth (of My message, the Kingdom) and the truth will make you free. And I am the way, the truth and the life." After validating them, it's important to bring the New Ager into an experience. This is the "and-you-will-know-the-truth" part. Maybe pray for them to feel the power of God. You certainly don't have to be religious about it. Maybe pray for an angel of God to come and reveal the Kingdom of God to them. It doesn't matter; all that matters is that they realize the world you live in is bigger than the world they've been living in. Bill Johnson says that "people will die thinking they have found true light unless True Light walks into the room."

Finally, introduce them to Jesus. It is Him they are really seeking. It is Him that they will find. This is the "and-the-truth-will-make-you-free" part. Every encounter with the supernatural, whether healing, angelic visitation, prophesy – everything – should point to Him. Jesus ended his encounter with this woman by saying, "I who speak to you am He" (John 4:26 NASB) concerning her comment about the "coming" Messiah.

I love New Agers, because they are already open to and experiencing the supernatural. That's half of the debate already settled. It's easier to sell a car to someone who already knows how to drive than to someone who has never even seen a road. So, again, I'm encouraging Christians not to immediately dismiss New Age claims of experiences with spirits, but instead to use the experiences to show them the Truth, the Way and the Life.

What gender are angels?
When it comes to this controversial question, I would have to agree with Dr. Grieg, who says,

> *"The evidence for angels manifesting themselves with female form as well as with male form may not be abundant but there is clear*

evidence in Scripture that this is the case, and the evidence is tied to a core doctrine of biblical theology, the doctrine of humanity created in the image of God as Father of all creation" (Grieg 2008:25).

The doctrine Grieg is referring to has its roots in Gen. 1: "Then God said, 'Let Us make man in Our image, according to Our likeness…God created man **in His own image**, in the image of God He created him; **male and female** He created them" (Gen 1:26a, 27 NASB, emphasis mine). From this, and several other passages (namely Isaiah 49:15 and 66:13) we know that God's image is both male and female. Actually, in Gen 17:1, when God establishes His covenant with Abraham, He introduces Himself as "God Almighty." This is the name *El Shaddai*, which is the All-Sufficient One. Literally translated, this word means "the God of many breasts." This proves Him to be All-Sufficient; having enough to be able to supply every need. There's much precedence for recognizing the "mother" heart of Father God. Grieg quotes Dr. Send-Kong Tan as saying the following:

"Echoing Justinian and Tertullian, Calvin…affirms that He is Father to both humanity and angels through Christocentric filiation [*Institutes,* 2:14:5, 488; 3:20:40, 903]…A doctrine of the *imago Dei* [image of God] that includes the angelic realm grounds for Christian angelology, as it should, within the doctrine of the trinity. For, when the Church proclaims that the 'one God' has created 'all that is seen and unseen,' she is affirming nothing less than a doctrine of angels, which is circumscribed within the Trinitarian structure and content of the Nicene Creed" (Grieg 2008:28).

So, if God is "the maker of heaven and earth, of things visible and invisible" (Nicene Creed), then surely He has created the angels. If He has created the angels, there is evidence of Himself in them. If there is evidence of God Himself in the angels, who's it to say that it is only of His masculinity?

In chapters 2 and 3 we have already spent a few pages talking about guardian angels, but here, I'd like to pose another question. If Peter's angel in Acts 12 was mistaken for actually being Peter, then what would a woman's angel look like? Why would we be so quick to assume that they would be "male-looking" angels?

Noted evangelist Billy Graham shares the following testimony in his book, Angels: God's Secret Agents:

Dr. S. W. Mitchell, a celebrated Philadelphia neurologist, had gone to bed after an exceptionally tiring day. Suddenly he was awakened by someone knocking on his door. Opening it he found a little girl, poorly dressed and deeply upset. She told him her mother was very sick and asked him if he would please come with her. It was a bitterly cold, snowy night, but though he was bone tired, Dr. Mitchell dressed and followed the girl.

As *Reader's Digest* reports the story, he found the mother desperately ill with pneumonia. After arranging for medical care, he complimented the sick woman on the intelligence and persistence of her little daughter. The woman looked at him strangely and then said, "My daughter died a month ago." She added, "Her shoes and coat are in the clothes closet there." Dr. Mitchell, amazed and perplexed, went to the closet and opened the door. There hung the very coat worn by the little girl who had brought him to tend to her mother. It was warm and dry and could not possibly have been out in the wintry night.

Could the doctor have been called in the hour of desperate need by an angel who appeared as this woman's young daughter? Was this the work of God's angels on behalf of the sick woman? (Graham 1975:2-3).

We cannot ignore Zecheriah 5. It is in this unique passage that Zechariah has a vision where he sees two women who "were coming out with the wind in their wings; and they had wings like the wings of a stork..." (Zech. 5:9). Now, the Bible never explicitly says that these women are angels, but we should be able to conclude that from what the text says.

I think this is another example of us needing to – and not being afraid to – reason it out with God. I do agree with Dr. Grieg's analysis. He also notes that "the burden of proof is on those who claim that angels may only assume male forms; such a claim fails entirely to explain the assumption about guardian angels in Acts 12:15, and it fails to explain the dual male-female reflection of God's image in the humans that guardian angels may manifest themselves to resemble" (Grieg 2008:30).

Do angels have free-will?

This was covered in an earlier chapter, but I felt the need to include this topic here to go into it in more depth.

Angels have some form of what David Reagan calls self-determination. "That is," he writes, "they have the freedom to remain in that holy estate into which they were placed by creation or to leave their first estate for a lower one" (Reagan [2008]:1.3). This he understands from Jude's letter, verse 6: *"And angels who did not keep their own domain, but abandoned their proper abode..."*(NASB) They chose to leave their territory. So the third of heaven (note: it's not a third of the angels, it's a third of heaven) that left with Satan made that choice.

Concerning salvation, Peter wrote about what we've been given through Jesus Christ, and they are things "angels **desire** to look into" (1 Pet. 1:12, NKJV, emphasis mine). This verse implies that angels have a will – self-determination – to see into something.

Also, how could Lucifer rebel against God without having his own thoughts and decisions?

> *How you have fallen from heaven, O star of the morning, son of the dawn! You have been cut down to the earth, you who have weakened the nations! But you have said in your heart, "I will ascend to heaven; I will raise my throne above the stars of God, and I will sit on the mount of assembly in the recesses of the north. I will ascend above the heights of the clouds; I will make myself like the Most High" (Isaiah 14:12-14 NASB).*

Notice how often the star of the morning (Lucifer) says "I will." These five "I wills" are an angel of God making unfortunate decisions for himself. So, to answer the question: yes, angels have a free-will and are capable of making decisions. However, the angels that remain have chosen to obey Psalm 103:20-22, which brings us to the next question...

Can we command angels? Are we supposed to give them orders?
Psalm 103:20-22 says,

*Bless the Lord, you His angels, mighty in strength, **who perform His word, obeying the voice of His word.** Bless the Lord, all you His hosts, **you who serve Him, doing His will.** Bless the Lord, all you words of His, in all places of His dominion; Bless the Lord, O my soul!" (NASB) (emphasis mine).*

To answer the question: No, I do not believe that angels will just obey our commands, as if we were to order an angel to cook us dinner or pick up our dry-cleaning. But Psalm 103 is clear about one thing: they obey the "voice of His word." Notice it doesn't say that the angels obey His voice, but the "voice of His word."

Throughout scripture and history, we understand that God has different ways of communicating to us. Hebrews 1 says that God spoke in "many portions and many ways." Often, He uses man's own mouth to convey His messages. So what would the "voice of His word" sound like? Well, have you ever prophesied? Have you ever recounted a Bible verse that was needed for the moment? Matthew 18:10 tells us that angels continually see the face of the Father. They are familiar with Him. They know His character, smell, color, sound, feel, and even taste. Well, when you release the "voice of His word," if it's from the Lord, an angel will recognize the smell, or sound, or taste of heaven coming from your lips. It doesn't matter where the voice is coming from, only that the angel recognizes it as the "voice of His word."

One of our GSSM graduates and house church leaders, Michelle, has an interesting story about her father, who was not saved at the time. She had just heard a teaching about asking God to dispatch angels. Later, when she saw her father, they were arguing about God, and Michelle was getting kind of frustrated. Remembering the teaching, she thought to herself, *God, would You dispatch the angels to come and show my dad that You're real.* No sooner had she said that when her father went sideways into the drywall. An angel had literally picked up her father and thrown him in the wall! Needless to say, eventually Michelle's father got saved.

Notice how Michelle spoke the word. She did not say, "Hey, angel, pick up my father and throw him into the wall." Nor did she say, "Angel, God showed me you were going to do this, so do it!" Instead, she asked God. She did not even address the angel! But what happened? The angel heard <u>her</u> voice, but recognized <u>God's</u> command in it, and acted. Remember, angels are ministering spirits come to serve the heirs of salvation. They're on our side! You will remember the words of Davi Silva at the beginning of this chapter. "You don't have to command a friend."

In the Old Testament, we see several instances where requests were made of angels that they didn't comply with. In Judges 13, Manoah asks the visiting angel of the Lord to reveal his name, and he refuses to. And the angels who went to Sodom and Gomorrah certainly negotiated and cooperated with Abraham and Lot. But they did not hesitate to carry out their commands and powerfully take Lot and his family out of Sodom in Genesis 19.

Lastly, Psalm 91:11 says in the NIV, "For he will command his angels concerning you to guard you in all your ways." All we're responsible for is speaking the word of the Lord, whether it be Scripture, prophesy, declarations, or even tongues. God will do the rest!

What happened in Genesis 6? Did angels, fallen or holy, come to the earth and impregnate women? Who, or what, are the Nephilim?

Let's take a look at the passage in question:

Now it came about, when men began to multiply on the face of the land, and daughters were born to them, that the sons of God saw that the daughters of men were beautiful; and they took wives for themselves, whomever they chose. Then the Lord said, "My Spirit shall not strive with man forever, because he also is flesh; nevertheless his days shall be one hundred and twenty years." The Nephilim were on the earth is those days, and also afterward, when the sons of God came in to the daughters of men, and they bore children to them. Those were the mighty men who were of old, men of renown (Gen 6:1-4 NASB).

It is after this that God decides to "blot out man from the land," and we know that familiar story about Noah and the ark. The above passage, however, has several different possible interpretations. I will not attempt to say, "This one is right, and that one is wrong," because first of all, I'm not sure myself. I have my opinion, but I will only present to you the different views and possibilities, and let you make your own decision (or not) on what you think happened in Gen 6.

The different interpretations of this passage come from different interpretations of the phrase, "sons of God." Well known author and biblical scholar H.L. Ellison writes of the phrase:

"This term is used in the OT only of angelic beings, perhaps of higher rank. It was only because the possibility of sexual relationships contradicted the general concepts of angels, that early rabbinic expositors understood it to mean personnel of high social class, i.e. there was a disregard of social differences, and very early the Church Fathers, followed by many of the Reformers, referred it to the descendants of Seth (so Leupold). The earliest Jewish interpretation was of angelic beings" (Bruce 1979:120).

Even Ellison admits that it was because of a challenge to the "general concept" about angels that the meaning of this word changed. This brings us to our first viewpoint...

Angels View

There are some who maintain that the phrase "sons of God" always refers to angels. In Job 1:6 and 2:1, we learn that the "sons of God" present themselves before the Lord. It is by no stretch that we understand the "sons of God" here to be angels, perhaps a higher form like Ellison suggested, because they stood before God. Even Job 38 mentions them, saying that "all the sons of God shouted together" when the morning stars sang together. Here, it is assumed that because the same terms are used, the meaning is the same. The other citing of the phrase is found in Hosea 1:10, where it is prophesied that it will be said of Israel that "You are the sons of the living God." In this case, it's clearly not talking about angels, but about the Israelites. Advocates of the angel view argue that different forms (singular vs. plural) of the word "God" are used here, therefore having different meanings.

So, if "sons of God" refers to angels three times in the book of Job, does that mean it must refer to angels in the book of Genesis? Not necessarily so. The same phrases do not always have the same meaning when they are used in different places in Scripture. For example, in Ezekiel, the phrase "Son of Man" refers to the prophet Ezekiel, while in the Gospels it refers to Jesus. Am I saying the angels view is therefore invalid? No... merely that it is hard to come to a firm conclusion on this issue.

Another part of this view is that these are fallen or unholy angels. Jude 6 -7 says,

> *And angels who did not keep their own domain, but abandoned their proper abode, He has kept in eternal bonds under darkness for the judgment of the great day, just as Sodom and Gomorrah and the cities around them, since they in the same way as these indulged in gross immorality and went after strange flesh, are exhibited as an example in undergoing to punishment of eternal fire. (NASB)*

Here, Jude writes to us about these fallen angels, saying they did not keep their own domain, but they "indulged in gross immorality and went after strange flesh." Could this be the "sons of God" going into the daughters of men? Perhaps it was this act that got them thrown out of heaven, because we understand from Jude that it was by an act that the angels "abandoned their proper abode."

This theory would make sense when you consider the Nephilim. This is not the only time you read about these giants in scripture. When Moses sent the twelve spies into Canaan, they came back and reported the following:

> *They gave out to the sons of Israel a bad report of the land which they had spied out, saying, "The land through which we have gone, in spying it out, is a land that devours its inhabitants; and all the people whom we saw in it are men of great size. There also we saw Nephilim (the sons of Anak are part of the Nephilim); and we became like grasshoppers in our sight, and so we were in their sight" (Num. 13:32-33 NASB).*

Where would these giants come from? Where could they have come from? Fallen angels impregnating women would certainly answer a lot, but is that even possible? In Matt. 22:30, Jesus says, "For in the resurrection they [men and women] neither marry nor are given in marriage, but are like the angels in heaven." It is reasoned that if angels will never marry, and if there is a finite number of them and no more will be created, then they will not have reproductive organs like men and women do. However, Jesus' words are about marriage, not necessarily sexual relations.

Tyrants view

In an article by Thomas Howe, he writes:

"This view claims that the phrase "sons of God" in Genesis 6 refers to male humans who were possessed by demons. If the term "sons of God" does not refer to angelic beings (demons), however, then there is no reference to them in the text at all. These interpreters assume the involvement of fallen angels being from the angels view and smuggle the assumption into the text while eliminating the only term that could refer to them. This is called "begging the question": the conclusion is assumed and used as part of the argument" (Christian Research Journal 2004:27.3).

Howe is right: to use the phrase as anything other than defining angels revokes the right to imply that angels were involved at all in the passage. Which brings us to our last view:

Line of Seth View

Says Howe,

"Advocates of the "line of Seth" view assume that the identity of the "sons of God" in Genesis 6 should be determined from its context before appealing to Job or Jude. This view holds that the "sons of God" refers to the descendents of Seth, while the "daughters of men" refers to the descendents of Cain. In other words, the righteous line of Seth intermarried with the unrighteous line of Cain resulting in the corruption of society" (Christian Research Journal 2004:27.3).

Steven Brooks says that the "sons of God" in Gen. 6:2 is explained for us in vs. 3. "Then the Lord said, 'My Spirit shall not strive with man forever, because he also is flesh; nevertheless his days shall be one hundred and twenty years'." Brooks defines the "sons of God" as being men who strive against the Spirit of God.

"The sons of God refer to the natural descendants of Seth who were godly men, yet they succumbed to carnal desires and begin to marry ungodly women. These women are identified as the "daughters of men," which refers to those women who were descendants of Cain, the man who murdered his brother" (Brooks 2007:39).

Genesis 5:1-3 follows an interesting lineage. It says that God created Adam in the likeness of God, and that Adam became the father of Seth, who was according to Adam's image, and in Adam's likeness. That is not said about any other in Adam's lineage. So, we can understand that through Seth, the line of the "sons of God" is continued. This view, however, gives no solid explanation for the Nephilim, these giants and mighty men of old and renown.

These are the three major views. Which one is right? I don't know. I suppose we will have to learn the answer to this one in "the age to come."

There is a lot of talk about "territorial" spirits, as in demons over regions. Are there angels who are over territories and regions?
There is much talk about evil principalities and territorial spirits. Instead of focusing on that, however, I'd like to focus on the fact that Satan, who cannot create anything, based the hierarchy of hell on heavens. So, it follows, that when there is a counterfeit, there is also the genuine article. Revelation tells us about such angels:

After these things I saw another angel coming down from heaven, having great authority, and the earth was illumined with his glory. And he cried out with a mighty voice, saying, "Fallen, fallen is Babylon the great! (Rev. 18:1-2a NASB).

Here, the writer John distinguishes this angel from others by saying it has great authority. In his book, Angelic Encounters, James Goll conjectures the following:

"Such angels of great authority perhaps rule over spheres of authority on the earth, such as cities and regions. Clement of Alexandria, an early Greek theologian, seems to have believed this was true. Referring to Daniel 10:13-21, he wrote, 'The presiding powers of the angels have been distributed according to the nations and the cities'" (Goll 2007:63, quoting *The Coptic Church and Dogmas* [2006]:3.2).

Isaiah 44:7 teaches us that God "established" the nations. When He sets a nation in place, He places an angel to watch over that nation. While on Global Awakening's annual Power Invasion trip to Brazil, I encountered the angel over Brazil in an open vision. This angel was huge and stood over the whole country. He was dressed in blue, green and gold, just like the flag of the nation. Even his hair was gold. In this vision, this angel hurled a spear towards the center of the nation, not for judgment, but to revive the nation's heart. I knew it was Brazil's angel not only because of its clothes, but because the spear was a "spear of authority," that was sharp on one end, but had the Brazilian flag tied to the other end.

Goll continues,

"In a similar way, it is likely that churches have angels assigned to them. We think of the phrase "to the angel of..." before the names of each of the seven churches in the Book of Revelation, chapter 2 and 3. Each of the seven utterances begins in the same way: "And to the angel of the church [in/of]..." Ephesus, Smyrna, Pergamum, Thyatira, Sardis, Philadelphia, and Laodicea... "write..." Specific, pointed messages of both encouragement and rebuke are given. What would the angels of these churches do with these words? Why would John be like a messenger to the angels of these churches? Were these words addressed to actual angels, to human overseers of the churches, or to the prevailing spirit of each church – or to a combination of these possibilities? This is another case where we have more questions than answers" (Goll 2007:62).

One thing, however, is clear: "As for the mystery of the seven stars which you saw in My right hand, and the seven golden lampstands: the seven stars are **the angels of the seven churches**, and the seven lampstands are the seven churches" (Rev. 1:20 NASB, emphasis mine).

Here is something to consider: are "nations" limited to physical locations and regions? When the Bible talks about "nations," could it mean more than that? Online social networks like MySpace and Facebook have been sprouting up all over the world-wide web since 2004. As of January 2008, the Facebook community has over 60 million users, and has been growing at a rate of 250,000 new users per day since January 2007. MySpace has over 110 million active users, and has become a household name in this country and much of the world (http://techradar1. wordpress.com/2008/01/11/facebookmyspace-statistics/). In my opinion, this compromises a nation. A massive one, at that. Am I saying that MySpace has an angel assigned to it? No, I'm merely thinking about the possibilities. What about political parties? Or worker's unions? I don't know that we can ever answer these questions in this age, but it certainly gives us something to think about.

CHAPTER 5

ANGELIC ENCOUNTERS:
THEY ARE FOR YOU TOO!

"Everything you say tonight will happen". That was the sentence that changed everything for me. I had only been at our school (GSSM) for a year. I had left a career in social work as a school social worker. When I came to the school I knew "there had to be more", I just didn't know where to find it. I came to the school needing to see more of the power of God. I was hungry to understand his ways. After one year of the school, I went on Global Awakening's annual Youth Power Invasion, the same trip Brandon had gone on a few years earlier. This is the account of one of the nights of ministry on that trip.

It was the second week of the annual Youth Power Invasion, in July of 2007. The youth were all split into teams and working at different churches all over Sao Paulo, Brazil. I was with a team of twelve U.S. youth, and for some reason that night four additional Brazilians had decided to come with me. Little did I know that one of those four had been imparted, and released into an incredible gift that would change my life forever. Suzanna was only seventeen and had been prayed for three nights earlier by Davi Silva. Davi is one of the leaders of Casa de Davi, a prayer and worship ministry in Londrina, Brazil. Davi carries an incredible impartation of seeing in the spirit realm, specifically toward the angelic. Since that night, Suzanna had been able to see angels clearly, with open eyes. She did not see with impressions, but rather in a literal sense, as if they were standing in front of her.

That night I was with my team at a small church of about 400 people. I had felt earlier that God had shown me that we were all going to get personal angels that would minister with us. As I said this to my team, who were all sitting in a circle around a table, Suzanna began to laugh. She said "As soon as you said that angels came into the room and began to stand behind each person sitting down. The biggest one is standing behind you, and he has swords for hands. God is saying that He is here, so that everything you say tonight will happen". At that moment I began to feel burning heat run up and down the right side of my body. I knew that tonight would be different.

The service started as usual with worship, but there was one exception. Suzanna would tell, as in play-by-play, what the angels were doing. Some were standing, but most were dancing. She would laugh as she would tell me with clarity how they were interacting with the worship. Although I could not see them, I knew they were there. This night was different than the night before. There was a different feel to the atmosphere. Even though she had told me of the angels, and the promise of God, I asked God to give me a sign that what he had spoken through Suzanna would actually come to pass. As I was asking, I began to feel raindrops splash on my arm. As I looked down there were raindrops falling on my Bible. I carefully looked around, at the ceiling and at those around me. There did not seem to be a leak in the ceiling or a puddle anywhere else in the room. God then said to me, "You asked for a sign, what do you think this is?"

Even with all of that confirmation, I was still reserved and unsure as I walked up to the microphone to begin the message for the evening. As I stood up, I began to feel the fire on my right side again. I tried to ignore it, launching into a message about faith and the power of God. How ironic, that God was giving me some of the very things that He had created to release His power, and to partner with our faith, and here I was trying to deny them.

As I continued to speak the heat intensified. Finally, I could not stand it anymore. I stopped my message and said:

"There are angels here tonight, and they have come to make the impossible happen. Right now there is an angel standing on my right side and he has lit it on fire. Now he is setting my head on fire. There is the power of God in this place. He has released his angels like flames of fire to come and release His power tonight".

The entire time I was talking Suzanna was whispering to her sister. She would later tell me that the angel was standing by me, but that it would not act until I confirmed what was happening. Then, almost as if in unison, the angel would do what I would describe, setting my right side on fire, and then moving to my head. While I was describing to the church what the angel was doing, God highlighted three young men to me. I pointed to them, saying, "God has called you to be like Shadrach, Meshach, and Abednego. He is going to put you in the fire of his furnace so you will know how to stand, and not bow". Suzanna informed me later that as soon as I said that the angel moved with several others and began to set the young men on fire.

This pattern of calling things out and releasing the power of God, with confirmations of angelic activity, was a constant for the night. As the night continued there were 27 that accepted the Lord as their Savior and there were countless healings. Every person I prayed for was healed, including breast cancer (doctor's reports later confirmed that). This was true for many of my team members as well. U.S. youth, who were there to serve Jesus, learned a powerful lesson on partnering with the angelic that many seasoned believers have yet to experience. This night changed my life forever. It provided a key to me regarding healing and the release of God's power through partnering with angels. It sent me on a path that many believers are currently interested in traveling....one of encounter. Since that time I have had other angelic encounters. I have continued to learn how angels partner with us to release healing and a divine touch from God. It has been the most amazing journey of my life. Now I am seeing angels, as well; at times with the same clarity as Suzanna. I am convinced that this is in large part due to the fact that even though I could not see the angels that night in Brazil, I honored their presence. Because of that, I have grown "spiritual eyes" to see more clearly!

The remainder of this chapter will deal with angelic encounters: how to have one, what to do with it once you have it, and how to interpret it. This chapter is going to give you an understanding about angelic encounters that you personally can experience. This is not a "how to" guide, but more is based on biblical and historical precedent. For many years angelic visitation has been held at arms length by believers. From history, we know that there was a time when angels were so common that they did not evoke a startling reaction. When Peter was mistaken for an angel, the other disciples did not have any type of strong reaction. Rather, they offered an explanation of Peter's arrival that seems unnatural to us. Most Christians today would say "how did you get out?" Their assumption was that an angel must be at the door. This type of environment is not just for the disciples It is also for us as well. Can we get to a place where encountering angels again is part of "normal Christian life"? Yes! Not only can it happen, but it will happen. We as believers can "tap" into the experience of engaging with the heavenly realms so that it becomes a consistent and clear point of contact. With that in mind, let's dive into the world of personal angelic encounter.

Can I Expect A Visitation Of An Angel?

Many people have a problem with accepting the fact that they can expect a visitation by an angel. In earlier chapters there was a biblical foundation laid concerning why we can expect this type of heavenly interaction. There have been many examples from both the Old and New Testament pointing to the fact that angelic visitation should be a part of our life. Just as the church is beginning to turn to healing, feeling and experiencing the power of God, it should also have an expectation of an increase of angelic experiences and encounters. We could say that believers have been experiencing some degree of angelic encounter all along, but just have not realized it. Hebrews 13:2 warns, "Do not neglect to show hospitality to strangers, for thereby some have entertained angels unaware" (ESV). I would be saddened if I had an encounter with an angel and had somehow missed it. Hopefully, this chapter will create a hunger to be aware of the possibility of such visitations, so as not to miss this divine connection from God.

Often when talking about having a visitation or encounter people want a formula or a mode for how to engage in this type of relationship. While there are some things that believers can do to "position themselves" for an encounter, throughout history there are many encounters that just happen to men and women of God.

Do I Have A Role In A Visitation or Encounter?

As mentioned earlier, the answer here is both yes and no. Law states this in his book regarding activating angels:

"I hesitate to say 'activating' angels since that term has been misused in recent years to imply that angels are our servants, not just fellow servants of God. However, used in the sense that we can make it possible for them to help us, activating is an accurate term. They stand by watching, "unactivated," if we are not "on the right road" at the right time and place.

Essentially, angels are agents of the government of God, the Sovereign Ruler of the universe (Is. 46:8-11; Rom. 11:36; Eph. 1:11). Activities of angels in the Bible were directly related to God's sovereign plan." (T. Law 1994:197)

These are five ways you can personally steward a visitation of an angelic presence.

1. Obedience And Yieldedness Is Key

It is essentially the role of the believers to put themselves into a state of obedience or yieldedness. This opens up the atmosphere the believer is walking in to come into alignment with the specific assignment or commission on that angel. When those two happen in convergence there is an opening for an encounter. This is important to remember as well in the terms of honoring the Spirit. Many times the Spirit is prompting us to come into alignment with what God is doing, but we are afraid to take a risk and go for it. If we began to listen more to the voice of the Spirit instead of the voice of fear, there may be more modern day angelic encounters.

2. Worship Sets The Stage

Earlier there was a discussion about angels being attracted to the worship of the saints. Many other heavenly beings derive their purpose from worshiping around the throne and the glory. If there is a call on earth for that same atmosphere to manifest, it would make sense that angels would be attracted to that. Also as previously stated, angels are fellow servants of God. Wherever the name of God is elevated there is a natural attraction for the angelic.

In many instances I have gone into worship times inviting the presence of God and the angels to come to partner with the release of healing power. I have watched as angels have come and touched those attending a service with sovereign healing. At a recent School of Healing and Impartation meeting in Ohio one of our Global School of Supernatural Ministry students saw angels with healing virtue for nerve disorders enter the room. As we continued to worship, many were sovereignly healed of paralysis, chronic headaches, pinched nerves, and even blindness.

Angels know that they are not to be worshiped, but when they recognize an atmosphere that is similar to that which exists in God's throne room, they come, with true healing in their wings.

3. Sacrifice and Honor Open Up The Ladders

The possibility of angelic visitation today is greatly increased through expressions of honor. We know that the sacrifice of Jesus on the cross allowed for the same ladder on which the angels ascend and descend (John 1:51) to manifest in us. Christ living in us gives us access to the same open heaven that Jesus had (Col. 1:27). That ladder however, is not open if we do not honor what God has prepared for us. Christ dwelling in us gives us access to something extraordinary, but if we do not honor that access, then there is no value for it in our lives. We honor what we place value on. That night in Brazil, I learned how to honor the little impressions, or sensing of angelic activity. Because of that, the entire church was blessed by multiple healings and encounters with the fire of God. By honoring the sacrifice of Christ, and the access he purchased for us, we give opportunity for the ladders of visitation to become more viable.

4. Ask In Prayer For The Hidden Things To Be Revealed

Prayer is a necessary key to angelic visitation. Many people talk about wanting to encounter angels, but when you ask them if they have asked for encounters, they will most likely tell you "no". Jeremiah 33:3 tells us to ask for the hidden things. If an angelic visitation is hidden, if it has not been revealed yet, then it's time to ask for it. By simply finding verses on angelic encounters, and on the hidden things being revealed, you are engaging God to set you up. Imagine what would happen if we would spend more time praying and less time trying to "work up" a visitation. Who knows, we might just get surprised.

5. Giving In Honor

There is one final key to angelic visitation. Giving can act like a status report for our focus. Law says on giving and angels, "Our stewardship in finance demonstrates probably more than anything else whether we have come under God's authority. The angels are aware of how we handle our money" (T. Law 1994:206). Authority is also another way of saying honor. When you are submitted to someone's authority, you are honoring him or her. Where a person sows, their money is a sign of what they value. This is not to say that the bigger the financial sowing the more angelic visitations. It is simply a principle of sowing and reaping. The same can be true for time, prayer or devotion. The same field in which we sow will be the field from which we reap. When desiring to live a life open to encounters, honoring God with acts of giving (sowing) is a part of devotion.

To summarize what has just been said, these are five basic keys that can be practiced to live a life expectant for visitation:

1. Obedience and yieldedness is key
2. Worship sets the stage
3. Sacrifice and honor open up the ladders
4. Ask in prayer for the hidden things to be revealed
5. Giving in honor

In his book, Engaging the Revelatory Realm of Heaven, Paul Keith Davis says this about coming into alignment for a visitation:

"To breakthrough victoriously requires diligence and determination through fervent prayer and intercession; not striving but conditioning" (P. K. Davis 2003:81).

When there is no breakthrough, it is time to fight for what is rightfully yours. Prayer and intercession can break open a heaven that should already be open, but may not be activated in your life.

What to do when a visitation happens:
There are four very important questions to consider when a visitation occurs: 1) How do I engage? 2) How do I know it is happening? 3) How do I know it is from God? and 4) What is the purpose?

In recent accounts of angelic visitations that are told to me, people often talk about being afraid when the angelic visitation is happening. Have you ever woken up in the middle of the night, and you are very much aware of your surroundings and your heart is pounding in your chest? I would imagine that was often the case when angels showed up in the Bible. Often times the angel greeted the human with "don't be afraid", or "fear not". Why is this? Isn't the fear of God a good thing? Let's look at fear for a second.

What is Fear?

Most of us think of the fear of God as being a reverent and holy emotional response to Godly encounters. Genesis 20:11 Abraham references the fear of God. This word "fear" in the Hebrew is *yir'ah*. It means fear, terror, awesome or terrifying, fear (of God), respect, reverence, piety, revered. This is the same root word that is used when talking about the fear of the Lord in Isaiah 7. It is the same meaning that is often used when talking about being in the presence of the Lord. It describes the human response when faced with the awesomeness of God. There is truly a state of reverential awe that comes from being the presence of God. However, there are other types of fear that the Bible also describes.

Most people think that *reverent* fear is what they feel when there is an angel present. That may be the case sometimes, however when the command "Fear not" is issued, there is another type of fear present. Looking at the following Scriptures will help us discover one of the main hindrances to an angelic encounter.

Hebrews 12:21 discloses that Moses felt fear when he was in the presence of Mount Zion and the angels of God. Fear in that verse is derived from the Greek word *ekphobos,* which means to be stricken with fear or terror, exceedingly frightened, or terrified. There is a real and tangible fear that can come from such an intense encounter with God and his angels.

Yet still there is another kind of fear that comes with encounter. In Luke 2:9, the shepherds were surrounded by the Glory of God, and the angel came to announce the birth of Christ. The Bible says that they "were filled with fear". This word fear is from the Greek word *phobos*, which means fear, dread terror, that which strikes terror. *Phobos* is also the root of another word for fear, *phobeō*, which means:

    1) to put to flight by terrifying (to scare away)
        a) to put to flight, to flee
        b) to fear, be afraid
    2) to be struck with fear, to be seized with alarm
        a) of those startled by strange sights or occurrences
        b) of those struck with amazement
    3) to fear, be afraid of one
    4) to fear (i.e. hesitate) to do something (for fear of harm)

The fear that is associated with this angelic messenger visitation is not a reverent fear of God, but is one that might be better described as terror. In the very next verse the angel says, "Fear not" (Luke 2:10). He is not cautioning them to hold back their reverential fear of God. He is saying "Don't be terrified, don't run away, don't go into a state of shock!" The angel came to deliver an important message, but the first thing he must do is dispel fear, so that the purpose of his visitation is not missed.

Can you imagine waking up in the middle of the night with an angel at the foot of your bed? For most it would cause a little *phobos* fear to come on them. It is this exact fear that can keep us from a visitation.

There is another side to this fear issue. The same word used for fear in Luke 2, is the word used in I John 4:16-18.

So we have come to know and to believe the love that God has for us. God is love, and whoever abides in love abides in God, and God abides in him. By this is love perfected with us, so that we may have confidence for the day of judgment, because as he is so also are we in this world. There is no fear in love, but perfect love casts out fear. For fear has to do with punishment, and whoever fears has not been perfected in love. (ESV)

The same fear that cannot coexist with love, is that which the angel cautions against in Luke 2. There is something about the unseen and the lack of assurance we feel about the unknown that causes us to bow to fear. When the angel appeared to the shepherds it was well outside of their normal routine. They were stricken with fear. Where there is a lack of God's perfect love, that same paralyzing fear holds us back.

There is hope. When God's love comes and invades us, it deals with what has been a hindrance to experiencing all that God has for us. Angelic encounters are a way for God to communicate with us. But it is also a means for us to interact with Him in a way that He always intended for us. Hebrews 8:5 clearly states that we are living in only a "shadow of heavenly" things here on earth. We know that the bridge to the Father created by Jesus' death on the cross gave us access to all heavenly things. The problem is that most of us have yet to walk in the eyes of faith to attain what is available to us (probably mostly due to ignorance). We are not limited to a type and shadow (copy), but we can experience the reality of heaven. Perfect love is another gateway allowing us to engage fully in that realm. John and Paul understood this. Earlier, while we were laying a biblical foundation, John and Paul were highlighted for their growth and maturity in love and faith. What was true for them in entering into more supernatural encounters is still true for us today. The angels help to bridge the gap from the throne room to earth. It only seems fitting that God in his sovereignty would allow love (which is who He is – God is love) to be the primary bridge to a deeper relationship with Him.

To summarize:

1. Fear can keep us from angelic visitation, or from all that the angels want to release.

2. The angels warn us not to fear, so that they can deliver their message and we can receive it.

3. The same fear that holds us back from angels, is exactly what perfect love wars against.

4. Where perfect love is, fear isn't.

5. Where perfect love is, so is God, and so is our capacity to engage in and receive from angelic visitation.

If you want to engage, spend time allowing God's perfect love to be your center. When an angelic visitor comes to you, allow yourself to be consumed with love first.

Once you begin to have victory over the fear that can confuse and hinder it is important to remember these points.

1. **Stillness:** when encounters first start to happen most people lose track of what God is doing by feeling a need to *do something*. Really, it is the messenger from God that is doing, your job is to stay still, relax and engage.

2. **Focus:** As the intensity of encounter grows, some have lost focus on what the message is or the purpose of the encounter. When focus is lost there is a risk of being distracted by all that is going on and missing what God is trying to speak to you.

3. **Acknowledge:** Acknowledging the richness of the moment and the manifestation of the presence of God is a necessary step. When we take the time to acknowledge, usually by thanksgiving, we open ourselves to experience and receive all that is intended to be released to us.

As you embark, remember to stay rooted in love (Eph 3), and remain still, focus, and acknowledge. With that in mind, get ready for the next step in this journey.

How Do I Know It's Happening?

Concerning angelic visitations James Goll says this:

"The ministry of angels can have much to do with the way spiritual gifts are received and delivered. They may appear to you with open eyes or eyes closed, in dreams or in actuality. They may stand behind you and you be unaware of them, yet perceived by others. They may be seen, felt, heard, or simply acknowledged and welcomed by faith. God's angels are a way that He utilizes at times to release *'divine information and spiritual revelation.'*" (J.W. Goll 1996:17)

What allows one person to sense an angelic encounter may not be the same indicator for another. Many times when talking about supernatural experiences, because many are still new to understanding this type of activity, there is a tendency to copy other's experiences. While there is something positive about learning from the examples of others, it is also important to understand that no two people are alike and God responds differently to us all. This frees us up and takes the pressure off. My experience does not need to mimic yours and vice versa.

In 1978 a pastor from Boise, Idaho began to have the most amazing encounters. Rolland Buck, says this about the first night of his visitation:

"On the night of June 18, 1978, I went to bed at my usual time with no advance notice that something was about to happen which would change my entire life!

About three o'clock in the morning, I was abruptly awakened when someone grasped my arms and sat me right up in bed! The room was dark because the shades were pulled, but there was just enough light from outside so I could detect the outline of a huge being.

To say the least, I was frightened because he was so strong I couldn't free myself from his grip. My fear didn't last, however, because I quickly became aware of a supernatural presence, and it didn't take me long to realize that this heavenly being was an angel from God….[he] told me not to be afraid! Then he told me that God had sent him because the prayers of God's people had been heard, and he was to deliver the message that their prayers had not only been heard, but had been answered!" (C and F Hunter 1979:19)

By the time this book was written, Buck had engaged in 16 visitations, and these interactions continued. In the next two years there were an additional 12 visitations. All had messages to bring to God's people. Most of the visitations were anywhere from 2-4 hours long.

There are a few keys that we can glean from Buck's interaction. *First*, he immediately dealt with fear. *Second*, he recognized the angelic being and did not try to explain it away. *Third*, he listened. Sometimes the unknown can cause a panic to well up inside of us. Angels are messengers, or ministers of God. They are simply looking for the proper time to release what God has for us.

How Do I Know It's From God?

This question is probably the most important when engaging in angelic visitation. It is known that the angel of light is one of deception. This has been such a concern in recent years that Law says this: "In fact, probably 75 percent of what is being written, said and seen today about angels is probably satanic" (T. Law 1994:216). When that statement was written, there was a large influx of angelic encounters in the New Age community. Law goes on to state that believers need to overcome, or redeem this God-ordained part of life by living Revelation 12:11

And they conquered him by the blood of the Lamb and by the word of their testimony, for they loved not their own lives even unto death.

In order to conquer that in which the enemy is trying to triumph, it is essential to employ three keys: 1) Use the blood, 2) Use the word of the testimony, and 3) Love not your own life. When these three keys are active there is a baseline for assurance that our lives are open for a Godly heavenly visitation.

When these visitations occur there are some keys to discerning their impact. The following is a list of nine keys to discernment from James Goll. This is one of the best scales for evaluating any type of supernatural activity.

1. **Edification, consolation, exhortation:** Does the spiritual event build up the people of God? 1 Corinthians 14 gives proper guidance for the need for all things to be edifying.

2. **Agreement with the Bible:** Is there scriptural support or basis for what is happening? 2 Timothy 3:16, all Scripture is breathed by God, and He is the originator of both Scripture and supernatural experience. We should expect them to line up.

3. **Exaltation of Jesus:** All experiences from God's heavens should glorify Jesus, and point the way back to him. Revelation 19:10 gives a clear guide that angels also carry with them the constant testimony of Jesus.

4. **Good Fruit:** It is true that you can judge a tree by its fruit. When the Holy Spirit comes He produces a distinct fruit that is not tainted. There is no room for pride, arrogance, or hurt (Gal 5:22-23).

5. **Accurate Predictions:** If there is a specific prediction made, the test will be if the prediction comes true (Deut 18:21-22). This is not a simple yes or no answer. The person who encountered the prediction must also be considered in the delivery of the message or encounter. Some Old Testament prophecies about Jesus seemed to not come to pass because they were so long in coming.

6. **Accurate Predictions Must Turn People Toward God:** "A spiritual experience that gives an accurate glimpse into the future must also affect people positively, turning them toward God" (J Goll 2007:128). (Deut 13:1-4)

7. **Liberty Or Bondage?**: Does the overall encounter allow the person to walk in more freedom? Where the Spirit of the Lord is, there is freedom. (2 Tim 1:7)

8. **Life Giving Or Death Dealing?**: Did this event give spiritual life or death? Was something produced, or did dreams and vibrancy die? John 14:6 says that Jesus is the life. If he is the life, then there can be no death produced from him.

9. **Witness Of Truth:** The Holy Spirit will bear witness to your spirit, if we are seeking truth, and the Holy Spirit is a spirit of truth (John 16:13).

These nine elements of evaluating encounters are a necessary baseline. Not all of these keys will need to be met in every circumstance (if there is no prediction, there is no need to see if it comes to pass). In all of Rolland Buck's encounters with angels (Gabriel to be exact), only once did he quote Scripture. Buck asked the angel during the second visitation "Who are you", the angel responded, "I am mentioned in Luke 1:13-19" (S. B. White 1987:17).

What is the purpose?

At the end of every encounter it is important to ask the Holy Spirit to show you the purpose. Buck's life was marked by angelic encounters that commissioned him with a message for the church. Jesus had angelic encounters that came to strengthen him. Matthew 4:11 focuses on the ministry that angels brought to Jesus after he was tempted. In previous chapters we have covered different roles that angels have and their scriptural basis. Whatever occurs during an angelic visitation, be aware of what the purpose is and what God wants you to do with it.

After Buck's first encounter, the same angel came back to him. Pastor Buck had not delivered the message that the angel had commissioned him with. At the second visitation this conversation took place: "Pastor you haven't given the message that the Father told you to give!" Pastor Buck said, "Oh, but I will, I will!" He expected the angel to chide him, but instead he said, "The Father knows how you feel, and He will be with you, and help you to obey Him!" (S. B. White 1987:16). Whatever you do, walk humbly in obedience and love, for God himself has issued a promise that he will be with you.

Encounters in Action!

"It began as a normal Wednesday" (L. Sherraden 2006:36). This is how Lucas Sherraden begins his book, *When Heaven Opens*. Lucas has been a friend of Global Awakening for a few years now. His book is the account of a phenomenal event that took place several years ago while on a trip to Brazil. Lucas had an encounter with an angel that had such intensity, he was left in a state of shaking for over 24 hours.

The team was traveling with Randy from Brasilia to Annapolis. Lucas had been prayed for earlier by Bill Johnson from Bethel Church, and Gary Oates the author of *Open My Eyes, Lord*. Gary's eyes had been opened to see in the unseen realm on a previous International Ministry Trip to Brazil. Since that time, he has continued to see angels with his eyes open and to release an impartation for seeing in the spirit, as well. On this day however, it was Lucas' turn.

After arriving at a church in Annapolis, the entire ministry team was in a meeting. Lucas felt the Holy Spirit leading him to ask Kathi Oates to pray for him. He did not want to go to the front of the church where she was sitting, because he did not want to create a scene. At that moment, she got up and decided to move to the back of the room. She sat down close to him. Lucas moved to sit next to Kathi and she began to pray for him. As she did, this is an account of what happened. Lucas was no longer aware of his earthly surroundings, but only these events.

"I saw an angel of the Lord come toward me with a sword in his right hand. Light flashed from the sword – whether the light emanated from inside the sword or was from some external source – I do not know. The expression on his face was very benevolent, but as he walked toward me it suddenly changed. It was the reluctant look of someone who had to do something they really did not want to do.

He lifted the sword and swiftly and purposefully plunged the blade deep into my heart. As the blade entered my chest cavity to the hilt, I doubled over in pain, feeling it cut deep into my flesh. The pain was so intense I felt as though I had died. Then the angel's hand began to guide the sword around the circumference of my heart – not just once, but repeatedly. I felt as if he was circumcising my heart." Lucas goes on to describe how years of hurt and pain were being eradicated from his life. After this "circumcision", Lucas had another encounter with the angel. This time there was not a sword, but what appeared to be a supernatural flamethrower.

"The angel began directing fire toward me. He began to shoot fire onto my feet and said he was lighting my feet to run to the nations. As the flames touched my feet in this supernatural experience, my feet in the natural got uncomfortably hot." Hours later his feet were still hot. This particular sign of burning feet followed him wherever he shared this portion of the encounter.

"The angel began to move to other parts of my body lighting them on fire. The room was nice and cool, yet I was sweating profusely. The angel directed the flame thrower toward my hands. He said, "I am lighting your hands on fire to bring healing to the masses." Then, he directed flames toward my eyes, and said "I'm preparing your eyes to see the beauty of the King." He also said, "Gone are the days when doing what you know will suffice." He said that I would be able to see and know what steps I was to take. He told me that what I saw I would need to obey immediately. As my emotions surfaced, a wave of unworthiness hit me, but I wanted to receive all that the angel was saying and doing."

Lucas goes on to describe the angel leading him to an encounter with the Lord. As he was standing before Him, the Lord morphed into a lion and began to roar with such intensity that it shook his body! As the encounter continued, the angel led Lucas above the city of Annapolis. The angel showed him a large ball of fire that was waiting to be released over the city. The angel then showed Lucas a net that was stopping the fireball from falling. Written on the crisscross webbing of the net were the words **UNFORGIVENESS and BROKEN RELATIONSHIPS**.

This encounter had a profound impact on Lucas and his ministry. But it also had a profound impact on those around him. Lucas did not keep this encounter to himself, but honored what God had shown him by the angel and shared with everyone that he could. Because of this, God multiplied the meaning of the encounter to all those who heard of it.

Conclusion:
As we said at the beginning, this book is not an exhaustive study of the subject of angels but it is designed to whet your appetite for heavenly encounters. Hopefully by now, you have an increased hunger to engage the unseen realm and begin "entertaining" angels. It is likely that many of you have had angelic encounters but have not had the revelation to fully appreciate what was happening. Still others have desired to have one, but were at a loss as to how to begin. Armed with new insight and charged with a new sense of personal investment, you have come to understand

that the ladders are in place with much coming and going. Heaven is waiting. It is time to begin exploring a new realm. It is time to live in the purposes of what God has ordained for us along with these fellow servants of God.

WORKS CITED

Bentley, T. (2005). The Reality Of The Supernatural World: Exploring Heavenly Realms And Prophetic Experiences. Ladysmith, British Colombia, Canada: Sound And Fire Productions.

Davis, P. K. (2003). Engaging The Revelatory Realm Of Heaven. New Sutton, New Hampshire: Streams Publications.

Goll, J. W. and Goll, M. A. (2007). Angelic Encounters: Engaging Help From Heaven. Lake Mary, Florida: Charisma House.

Goll, J. W. (1996). Understanding Supernatural Encounters: A Study Guide. Grandview, Missouri: Ministry To The Nations.

Grieg G. (2008). Biblical Reasons to Receive God's Glory and Give It Away In Power Evangelism A Theological Response to Criticism of the Lakeland Outpouring and Todd Bentley. Regal Publishing Group. (http://www.cwgministries.org/books/A%20Theological%20 Response%20to%20Criticism%20of%20the%20Lakeland%20 Outpouring%20and%20Todd%20Bentley.pdf)

Grudem, W. (1994). Systematic Theology. Grand Rapids, MI: Zondervan House.

Hess, B. (2008). "Angels." Supernatural Phenomena [CD]. Global Awakening, Mechanicsburg, PA.

Hunter, C. and Hunter, F. (1979). Angels On Assignment. Kingwood, Texas: Hunter Books.

Johnson, B. (2003). When Heaven Invades Earth. Shippensburg, PA: Destiny Image.

Kaylor, M. (2010). The Journey of Supernatural Discovery. Coral Springs, FL: Rivergate Publishing.

King, P. (2002). Third Heaven, Angels, And Other Stuff. Belleville, Ontario, Canada: Essence Publishing.

Law, T. (1994). The Truth About Angels. Orlando, Florida: Creation House.

Sherraden, L. and Cooke, G. (2006). When Heaven Opens. U.S.A: Printed by Author.

Strong's Exhaustive Concordance. http://www.eliyah.com/lexicon.html. On-line reference for lexicons and Hebrew and Greek Scriptures.

White, S. B. (1987). The Man Who Talked With Angels. Green Forest, Arizona: New Leaf Press.

Williams, J. R. (1998). Renewal Theology. Vol. 1. Grand Rapids, MI: Zondervan House.

In "There Is More", Randy will lay a solid biblical foudation for a theology of impartation as well as take a historical look at the impartation and visitation of the Lord in the Church. This will be combined with many personal testimonies of people who have received an impartation throughout the world and what the lasting fruit has been in their lives. You will be taken on journey throughout the world and see for yourself the lasting fruit that is taking place in the harvest field - particularly in Mozambique. This release of power is not only about phenomena of the Holy Spirit, it is about its ultimate effect on evangelism and missions. Your heart will be stirred for more as you read this book.

"This is the book that Randy Clark was born to write."
- Bill Johnson